Nansen

Explorer and Humanitarian

Marit Fosse and John Fox

Hamilton Books

An Imprint of
Rowman & Littlefield
Lanham • Boulder • New York • Toronto • Plymouth, UK

Copyright © 2016 by Hamilton Books
4501 Forbes Boulevard, Suite 200, Lanham, Maryland 20706
Hamilton Books Acquisitions Department (301) 459-3366

Unit A, Whitacre Mews, 26-34 Stannary Street,
London SE11 4AB, United Kingdom

Library of Congress Control Number: 2015932743
ISBN: 978-0-7618-6578-0 (pbk : alk. paper)—ISBN: 978-0-7618-6579-7 (electronic)

All illustrations courtesy of the Archives of the League of Nations, Geneva.

Front cover: Dr Fridtjof Nansen, High-Commissioner for Refugees, sketched by Alois Derso. [Undated. Archives of the League of Nations, Geneva.] Alois Derso (1888–1964) and Emery Kelen (1896–1978) were two internationally recognized caricaturists who worked at the League of Nations for fifteen years. Both were of Hungarian Jewish origin and arrived in Switzerland after the First World War, where they drew humorous caricatures and political satires of the League of Nations delegates and politicians, as well as significant events such as the Disarmament Conference. Their work was published widely in the European press. Derso and Kelen departed Europe on 13 December 1938 aided by friends who recognized the impending dangers facing them due by both being Jewish and their past outspoken criticism of Hitler's rise to power.

∞™ The paper used in this publication meets the minimum requirements of American National Standard for Information Sciences Permanence of Paper for Printed Library Materials, ANSI/NISO Z39.48-1992.

Contents

Foreword

António Guterres,
United Nations High Commissioner for Refugees

Fridtjof Nansen was a pioneer in many ways—a scientist, an intrepid polar explorer, a respected diplomat. He was also the first High Commissioner for Refugees appointed by the League of Nations. In that role, he profoundly shaped the evolution of international efforts to protect some of the world's most vulnerable people—refugees who have been forced to flee their countries as a result of persecution and conflict.

Refugees have lost everything—their homes, their communities, their livelihoods, often even their loved ones. No longer under the protection of their own government, they depend on the generosity of other countries to provide them sanctuary and allow them to restart their lives without fear. As refugees, they enjoy a special legal status entitling them to "international protection" by their host countries. Fridtjof Nansen laid the groundwork for this system, spearheading early legal agreements that later became the basis for the 1951 Refugee Convention and UNHCR's work.

More than ninety years after Nansen was first appointed to assist Russian refugees in Europe, people continue to be uprooted from their homes every day. There are now more than 45 million people worldwide who fled violence and conflict, including over 15 million refugees and 29 million internally displaced persons. If they were a nation, they would make up one of the world's thirty biggest countries.

Nansen not only pioneered international work on behalf of refugees, he also embodied—already nearly a century ago—many of the fundamental tenets of humanitarian work. His greatest assets were his neutrality and political independence, and the confidence he as an individual inspired in others, irrespective of their national or political background. At a time when the political interests and positions of governments regularly disregarded the suffering of civilians, both Nansen's successes and his failures clearly illustrate a fact that still holds true today: humanitarian work is impossible without steadfast fidelity to the principles of neutrality, impartiality and independence. As humanitarian organizations work in crisis settings around the world, our ability to help people in need depends entirely on the credibility we have with all sides in a conflict—a credibility that is predicated upon our political neutrality. But at the same time, political independence and neutrality must not be translated to mean paralysis, and Nansen personified the ingenuity and perseverance in finding ways to push through solutions that mark an outstanding humanitarian.

Nansen paved the way for our refugee work, and his legacy remains with us today. In recognition of the importance of his efforts for international refugee protection, UNHCR has since 1954 presented its annual Nansen Refugee Award to individuals and organizations that have made exceptional contributions to the refugee cause. The award boasts a long list of laureates who share Nansen's personal conviction. Eleanor Roosevelt, who laboured for decades to champion open-door policies and refugee rights both within the United States and internationally. Graça Machel, the longtime activist who advanced protection norms for refugee children caught in the midst of conflict. Dr Annalena Tonelli, an Italian volunteer who fought against tuberculosis, HIV/AIDS and female genital mutilation among the forcibly displaced in Kenya and Somalia, and who ultimately sacrificed her life for her work. They, like Nansen, are true heroes of refugee protection.

This book is an important one. It portrays the many dimensions of a man who was one of the most interesting personalities of his time. And it shows, through that man's struggles, setbacks and overwhelming victories on behalf of hundreds of thousands of people in need, the fundamental importance of having a strong international system in place for their protection. This system now exists, also thanks to Fridtjof Nansen. But it continues to come under pressure, as respect for human rights runs low in many places, and as racism and xenophobia resurface, time and again, in societies around the world.

As UNHCR continues its work to protect and assist those who need it most, we are reminded each day that whether or not refugees can find safety and restart their lives depends, first and foremost, on the governments, the societies and the communities that take them in. Nansen recognized this, and worked with this knowledge to find creative, often unexpected solutions for refugees and people in need. I hope this book will help to spread this recognition, through the tribute it pays to one of the true humanitarians of all time.

Preface

When we worked together on our previous book about the League of Nations, we realised that much of the work that is currently being carried out by the international organizations is based upon the foundations laid during the 1920s.

Recalling the activities of the League of Nations today is not a fruitless activity given what is taking place on the international scene. For a long time, academic research has neglected this area where ideology and political reality confronted each other. When the League of Nations was dissolved on 18 April 1946, Lord Robert Cecil said: "The League is dead. Long live the United Nations." When the United Nations first saw the light of day, it was already clear that the League of Nations, for all its faults, was the ideological laboratory that had modelled, pioneered, even forged, the whole universe of the international world to come.

While the financial turmoil of 2008 was still sending shockwaves through the European countries and across the rest of the world, we realised that much of what we are living through today has similarities to what went on between the two World Wars. According to the United Nations High Commissioner for Refugees, the number of people in situations of displacement at the time of writing has reached 45 million—a fourteen year high. These figures include 15.4 million internationally displaced refugees, as well as 28.8 million people forced to flee their homes within their own countries. Some ninety years ago, Nansen did not blanch when confronted with what were for the time similarly daunting figures.

In difficult times we all need encouragement and see that action by an altruistic organization or, in this case, by a single man can make a tremendous difference. This is what we wanted to show by looking into the life of Fridtjof Nansen. When he found himself confronted with hundreds of thousands of prisoners-of-war isolated in Siberia everything had been lacking, except Nansen's fertile genius. Similarly, when faced with famine and millions of terror-stricken refugees, he showed what altruism can achieve when it is united with an indomitable will. He was a fighter; some persons may say an obstinate man but he put all his energy and efforts into helping other people. For all the years of toil he did not receive any salary. A true humanitarian.

Nansen was a charismatic character. He was an articulate speaker moved by a moral conviction for certain issues. In nearly everything he undertook Nansen introduced visionary and innovative ideas. As an outstandingly successful Arctic explorer, he went where few others dared to go using techniques that he copied from the natives of Greenland or invented himself. On the international scene, he insisted that prisoners-of-war, famine victims and refugees were matters of concern for the global community. Years ahead of his time, he even spoke of armed intervention by an international authority to protect threatened minorities.

We wish to take you on a journey back in history, and we hope that this book will give some encouragements to those who do have ideas, who want to put their imprint on this world. In order to achieve this they will need what Nansen possessed in large measure: perseverance, stubbornness, action.

We wish to thank David Chikvaidze, at the time Director of the United Nations Library in Geneva, for the support, encouragement and invaluable help he gave to us at each stage of this project. We are also deeply indebted to Jacques Orbeson and Lee Robinson for their valuable first-hand help and assistance. Alongside David Chikvaidze, we wish to thank the Archives Team of the League of Nations, especially Mrs Blandine Blukacz-Louisfert, without forgetting the kindness and support of the staff of the United Nations Library in Geneva—Carla Bellota, Pablo Bosch, Adriano Goncalves e Silva, Christina Giordano, Salvatore Leggio and Sebastien Vernay—who were of the greatest help to us,

Our particular thanks go to Carl Emil Vogt, a well-known specialist on Nansen. He read our manuscript, put us right on a number of points and very kindly allowed us to draw inspiration from his doctoral thesis. With his kindness, support and comments, we found ourselves deeply involved in this passionate historical tale.

A big "thank you" to all those who have supported us in this adventure.

Marit Fosse and John Fox

Chapter One

Nansen the Explorer

EARLY DAYS[1]

Fridtjof Nansen was a Norwegian scientist, explorer, oceanographer, artist, diplomat and humanitarian—a polymath. He was awarded the Nobel Peace Prize in 1922 for his work as the League of Nations High Commissioner responsible for repatriating prisoners of war from Europe and Central Asia in the aftermath of the First World War, for famine relief in Russia in 1921 and for initiating the new international concern for refugees.

Nansen belonged to the Norwegian "old society"—an upper class family with a long tradition of public service. He was brought up according to the ideals of an austere Protestantism and taught to respect hard work, duty and patriotism. His roots were in an elite social group displaying strong patriarchal behaviour, who saw themselves as nation-builders but with deep concern for the people they governed. They were opposed to the idea of "ignorant peasants" interfering in the reins of power, but in 1884 Norway introduced the parliamentary system and their worst fears were realised.

For both his mother and father, Fridtjof was a child of their second marriage. His father, Baldur Nansen, was a descendant of Hans Nansen, a famous mayor of Copenhagen in the seventeenth century. Baldur was a small, thin person, a lawyer and religious man with a clear conception of moral duty and responsibility. His first wife had died of puerperal fever. Fridtjof's mother had been born Wedel Jarlsberg into an aristocratic Norwegian family. When she met Nansen's father, she was known by her married name of Adelaide Bølling, having been left a widow with five children when her husband, an officer in the army, died of cholera. The couple met when Baldur became Adelaide's lawyer and they subsequently married. Fridtjof was this couple's first surviving son born in 1861 at Store Frøen, at that time on the outskirts of Christiana (as Oslo was known at that time by its Danish name); a brother Alexander was born one year later.

Thanks to his mother's encouragement, as a young man, Fridtjof became an expert skater, swimmer, skier and hunter and thus developed an excellent physique giving him great endurance and psychological self-reliance. At school he excelled at drawing and science. In fact, his interests and talents were so diverse that it was difficult to select a course of study for higher education. Finally, he decided to study zoology at the University of Christiana because he felt that fieldwork would involve working in the open air. Over the next fifteen years he would unite his athletic ability, his scientific interests, his yearning for adventure and even his talent for drawing in a series of brilliant achievements that brought him international fame.

In December 1881, Nansen passed "with distinction" the first-year university examination that allowed him to specialize. At this moment, however, the Department of Zoology at the University of Christiana required somebody to visit the Arctic to bring back some specimens of marine life. The only volunteer was Nansen, who found a berth on the new sealing vessel *Viking* which was leaving in March 1882 for Greenland, a largely unexplored region. On board the *Viking* he made notes on winds, ocean currents, ice movements, auroras and animal life. The commercial purpose of the voyage was to hunt for seal pelts and Nansen acted as a marksman on the hunting expeditions. Although the crew were disappointed with their season's hunting, after four months at sea Nansen came back with an extensive collection of zoological specimens, including polar bear skins and Greenland sharks.

However, upon seeing Greenland's icecap, he had conceived the ambition to be the first to cross it on foot, although it would take him six years to mount the expedition.

Upon his return, a lecturer at the university pointed out that the Museum of Bergen was looking for a curator in its zoological department. Although he was only 20 years old and had barely completed one year at university, Nansen was deemed suitably qualified and, after consulting his father, left for Bergen without delay for his first paid job.

At that time, Bergen was an isolated port accessible principally by sea from other Norwegian towns and where the people had their own particular dialect. It also had a changeable maritime climate, quite different from Christiana. Nansen became homesick and longed for the snow and forests of his homeland. In December 1882, he decided that he would ski home for Christmas alone with his dog for 250 kilometres across the mountains! He would make this trip several times on ski in winter or on foot in summer, describing his journey in a series of articles published in a Christiana newspaper. Nansen thus became a trial-blazer in the sport of cross-country skiing.

Marine biology was moving away from the classification of dead specimens towards the study of living creatures from the sea. Six months after taking up his post, the museum received the visit of a German zoologist who was interested in marine invertebrates. Following his lead, Nansen decided to specialize in the structure of the nervous system in lower marine life. Nansen lived in the age of scientific positivism implying a belief in biological evolution based on the ideas of Charles Darwin. If man really did originate from protozoa, as Darwin had suggested, the nervous systems of simple marine creatures could give a clue to the formation of human cell structure. For this work, he would need adequate equipment, so his father bought him the latest powerful microscope from Karl Zeiss. In order to depict accurately what he saw in the microscope, Nansen took up drawing lessons.

One particular feature of Nansen's life as a young man was the wearing of suits of "Sanitary Woollen Clothing" manufactured by the German tailor Dr Gustav Jaeger. These simple, light garments consisted of tight woollen trousers with a short jacket buttoning down the right side of the body with a breast pocket on the left. This, and the fact that he went clean-shaven and bare-headed on the streets of Bergen, set him apart among the other local characters.

Nevertheless, first he had to gain his doctorate. He was preoccupied with how nerve cells communicated with each other, but to understand more it was necessary to stain the tissues for examination by microscope. The best staining methods of the day were performed by Dr Camillo Golgi in Pavia, Italy. In March 1885, Nansen proposed to resign from the staff of the Bergen Museum in order to travel, but his superior, Dr Daniel Danielssen, refused to accept his resignation and suggested a year's leave with pay instead. It was in February 1886 that Nansen finally left Norway for Pavia in Italy. In a few days Dr Golgi showed him how his staining technique worked and then Nansen travelled on to the marine biological research station in Naples. Arriving unannounced, it took some time before the head, Professor Anton Dorhn, would accept him as a researcher.

Tall, blond and unmistakably Nordic, in Naples Nansen made a striking and attractive figure—particularly to wealthy, unattached, English-speaking ladies. He preferred the company of women and would make friendships in Italy that would endure all his life. Having arrived in Naples in April 1886, he was soon obliged to return to Norway for military service and by August was back in Bergen. He said of his trip to Italy: "I have never learned so much in such a short period of time."

In Naples he had completed his groundbreaking research on marine species, which was published in Norwegian in Bergen in the summer of 1886, and in English in September. He was not the only researcher working in this field but had the good luck to be the first to publish his findings. Although German was at this time the language of science, the following year Nansen published a larger book in English on the structure of the central nervous system with his own illustrations. His work was considered ahead of its time and he thus became one of the founders of neurology. An abridged translation of his book into Norwegian was presented as his Ph.D. thesis.

THE CROSSING OF GREENLAND

The end of the nineteenth century was a time when mankind was filling in the blanks on the Earth's surface. Livingstone and Stanley had thrown some light on the dark interior of Africa. There remained the Polar Regions and the unexplored ice-cap of Greenland. Nansen proposed an expedition crossing Greenland by travelling from the uninhabited east coast to the sparsely populated west coast—which meant that there would be no turning back.

In 1887, Nansen began to prepare in earnest for his expedition. An engineer in the United States Navy, Robert Peary, also had ambitions of crossing Greenland from coast to coast, but had been sent to survey a possible route for the future Panama Canal—thus, it was imperative for Nansen to act swiftly.

Nansen's first visit was to Baron Nordenskiöld in Stockholm, the acknowledged master of polar travel at that time. Nordenskiöld indicated that skis were the ideal method for traversing the Greenland ice-cap and, consequently, Nansen foresaw a small and fast-moving team of skiers pulling sledges. As his travelling companions he was joined by two army lieutenants and two Laplanders. The sixth member of the team was Otto Sverdrup, a farmer, sportsman and master mariner, who immediately became and remained Nansen's second-in-command for many years to come. The crossing was expected to take a month, so they took supplies for two months. A Danish businessman, Augustin Gamél, offered to finance the project, while transport to the Greenland coast was reserved on a sealing-ship, the *Jason*.

A feature of Nansen's expeditions was meticulous planning and foresight. Among the astute decisions he took was that the six men would sleep three together in two reindeer-skin sleeping bags so as to keep each other warm. Amongst the multitude of items carried by the expedition which were to prove invaluable were red-tinted glasses against snow blindness, two small-calibre twin-barrelled guns combining a rifle and shotgun, numerous bamboo poles, a wide selection of tools, sketch books, note books and a modern camera with rolls of film. Their scientific equipment included a theodolite, sextant, compasses, aneroid barometer, watches, thermometers, telescopes and something called a hypsometer which was a device to indicate altitude via the boiling point of water. Nansen had an open boat specially constructed with a double hull to resist the ice, which was equipped with tarpaulins, boat hooks, paddles, oars and a pump for bailing. Two items of equipment which were to prove inadequate for the extreme conditions of Greenland were the alcohol-burning stove and the tent. The stove burned methylated spirits which rendered alcohol unpalatable—Nansen was aware of the dangers of drunkenness—but it could never melt enough snow to quench their thirsts, which was a problem throughout the journey. Apart from its wooden struts, the silk tent consisted of separate elements—floor, walls, roof—and the wind easily penetrated every aperture filling the interior with fresh snow during blizzards.

Nansen had had five sledges constructed in Norway to his own specifications. They were strong, narrow, flexible and light, riding high above the snow. Four of the sledges measured about 3 metres long by 55cm wide and weighed about 12.5kg; the fifth one was slightly larger. The wood for the superstructure was ash, with the runners made of elm or maple. The sledges contained no screws or nails, the structure being held together by leather lashings—no repairs were required on the whole journey. However, the runners were strengthened by steel soles that were screwed in place.

A considerable part of Nansen's narrative of the expedition is concerned with food: what they took with them; how they prepared it; and even how they ate it. To save weight, it was obvious that dried food was the most suitable form of provision, so he planned a varied diet of dried meat, fats, dried bread and biscuit, with the addition of substances such as chocolate, tea, sugar and lemon powder. The added advantage of dried and powdered foods was that they did not freeze. He took as little as possible of "stimulants and narcotics" such as coffee and tobacco, and no alcohol whatsoever. As luxuries to be consumed when celebrating the achievement of milestones, they took some butter, dried fish, Gruyère cheese, oatmeal biscuits, jam and condensed milk. Once they reached the west coast of Greenland they were able to supplement their diet with fresh game, which they consumed with enthusiasm.

On 28 April 1888 Nansen successfully defended his doctoral thesis at the University of Christiana and four days later set off—very few people, particularly in the academic community, ever expected to see him alive again. Nansen observed that newspaper reports about his expedition were "distinguished by an astonishing ignorance" and a superstitious terror of the unknown. For the first part of their journey, the members of the expedition and their equipment were carried on board the Danish steamer *Thyra*, which docked in Scotland and the Faroe Islands before reaching Iceland.

The party then transferred its equipment to the *Jason* in a harbour of north-west Iceland and set sail for Greenland on 4 June. The plan had been to drop Nansen and his companions in a rowing boat offshore from where they would then approach the east coast of Greenland and find a landing place. A week later the mountain tops of Greenland were visible in the far-off distance but that year there was an unusually wide belt of pack ice which prevented the ship from getting anywhere near the coast. The captain of the *Jason* therefore began seal hunting while waiting for the situation to improve. Six weeks later the edge of the pack-ice was still twenty kilometres from the coast, so on 17 July Nansen and the captain of the *Jason* decided to launch the expedition's boat anyway. As well as Nansen's specially built craft, the captain gave them one of his own boats. The six men managed to penetrate to within a few miles of their intended destination at Cape Dan, but the pack ice proved to be too thick and they were unable to reach the shore. For the next two weeks they were obliged to drift helplessly along the edge of the pack-ice carried southward by the strong current "which rendered all resistance on our part completely futile." At the end of the month of July the ice began to break up and they were able to sail and row north again along the coast. Even so, they often had to force a passage through the ice with the help of axes and poles. From time to time they encountered friendly Eskimo[2] communities who, to the complete astonishment of the explorers, took all their clothes off when inside their dwellings. Finally, on 10 August they found an ice-free inlet, still about 150 kilometres south of their intended landing place and from the spot where the *Jason* had originally dropped them. They decided that this must be their departure point.

By 15 August they were ready to leave. For two days they had to haul the five fully-laden sledges up the initial steep ice slope on foot; with three men to a sledge, this obviously required several relays. Because the sledges would run better on a colder surface, they decided during this stage of the journey to sleep by day and travel by night (they were below the Arctic Circle, so there was no midnight Sun). After ten days of heavy uphill drudgery, they reached a height of about 2,000 metres above sea level and the slope began to ease. Even though they landed at the wrong place, Nansen's intention had still been to head for their original destination of Christianshåb (modern Qasigiannguit) on the west coast of Greenland several hundred kilometres to the north-west. However, given the prevailing wind blowing from that direction and the distance to be covered, on 27 August Nansen decided (to everyone's relief) to head due west for the settlement of Godthåb (modern Nuuk).

In general, the weather was good and the sun shone, but moisture in the air froze and fell to the ground in the form of fresh snow. Because of these conditions, the sledge runners encountered resistance and Nansen observed that the snow was "as sticky as sand." Thus, they could only advance a few kilometres each day over the interminable flat white surface, but by 1 September the slope had levelled off so that at last they could put on their skis and go more rapidly. The aneroid barometer eventually indicated a height of 2,777 metres above sea level. They began to suffer from snow blindness and dehydration. For the former they had red-tinted goggles, but the latter was not helped by their very inefficient spirit stove which could not melt enough ice and snow to slake their thirsts. Most of the time they had good weather and, now travelling by day, they suffered from sun-burn until they learned to protect their faces with red silk scarves.

By 6 September, they felt that the terrain was beginning to descend towards the west. Five days later they abandoned their biggest sledge and
redistributed the loads among the four others. They estimated by 17 September that they had covered a total of 300 kilometres and the going was definitely downhill. The wind now swung round behind them so that they were
able to mount sails on two sledges bound together and, with one man in front
and two behind on skis, sped along covering enormous distances at great
swiftness with no effort. After a number of mishaps, they also discovered
that the sledge's load had to be tied on very securely. On 19 September, they
were brought to a halt by the crevasses marking the west side of Greenland.
Two days later they found a pool of fresh water lying on top of the ice and for
the first time since the journey began were able to satisfy their prodigious
thirsts. By the early afternoon of 24 September they had with considerable
difficulty managed to find a way through the ice fall and descended to bare
land—the crossing had taken forty-one days. They abandoned their sledges
with part of their supplies and for two days walked down a valley towards the
sea carrying as much as they could.

They knew that they had arrived at Ameralikfjord, slightly to the south of
Godthåb, but there was no way of reaching the town by land. While Nansen
and Sverdrup started to make a boat out of bamboo poles and willow
branches covered by the groundsheet of their tent, the others went back to
recover the supplies left behind with the sledges. It should be noted that
Nansen and Sverdrup had already discussed the need to build such a boat
long before they reached the west coast of Greenland. Before the others got
back with the remaining provisions, Nansen and Sverdrup set off in their
improvised odd-shaped boat on 29 September. Four days later they reached
Godthåb. By chance they were met by the governor's assistant whose first
words were to congratulate Nansen on gaining his doctorate!

There was no telegraph at this time in Greenland and the last ship of the
year had already left in August; in fact, it had already left before they had set
out from the east coast. There was therefore no immediate way of signalling
to the outside world the success of their expedition. However, the Eskimos
arranged a relay of kayaks that brought the news 500 kilometres down the
coast to the mining settlement of Ivigtut (nowadays Ivittuut) where a merchant ship, the *Fox,* was waiting to sail. The kayakers caught the *Fox* just as
she was leaving harbour and news reached Norway on 9 November spreading like wildfire all over the civilized world.

The other four members of the expedition who had been waiting to be
rescued were soon brought to Godthåb among scenes of unprecedented cele-
bration. As it was so late in the season, everybody was now obliged to remain
in Godthåb for the seven months of winter. Nansen took advantage of this
time to study the Eskimo way of life, their language, their hunting techniques
and their clothing. He became an expert kayaker, knowledge which was

going to prove priceless in the coming years. Finally, on 25 April 1889 the Danish mailboat arrived and took them back to Copenhagen. The six explorers were greeted with a tumultuous welcome in Christiana on 29 May.

THE VOYAGE OF THE *FRAM*

In contrast to a number of disastrous polar journeys, Nansen's Greenland expedition achieved almost exactly what it set out to do without any loss of life. With the exception of the spirit stove and tent, the food and equipment were entirely adequate to the task, while the physical skills and fitness of the men showed how future polar expeditions should be organized. He was said to have launched a new era in polar exploration.

"Nansen fever" swept Norway. The Museum of Bergen wanted him to return to work there, but he was offered the post of curator of the zoological collection at the University of Christiana. This was a post with a salary but no work—a sinecure that seemed to suit everyone.

Still wearing his ever-present Jaeger suit, Nansen travelled to London to give a lecture at the Royal Geographical Society and was presented to the Prince of Wales, who would in the future become his good friend King Edward VII. Then on 11 August 1889 he became engaged to Eva Sars and less than a month later they were married. She was a 31-year-old singer, small with dark brown eyes and black hair and, according to Nansen, "the best woman skier in Norway." Nansen was to prove a tyrannical and moody husband prey to an unpredictable temper who ruled his wife and children with a firm hand, constantly calling for domestic economy. When they grew up, all his children had acquired painful memories of their harsh childhoods.

1891 saw the publication of his book *The First Crossing of Greenland* in English, German and Norwegian.

His next grand adventure, already announced on 18 February 1890, was to drift across the North Pole in a ship deliberately marooned in the pack ice. In 1884 the wreckage had been discovered in southern Greenland of a ship called *Jeannette* which had been crushed in the ice off northern Siberia in 1881. Nansen realised that if a ship could be built whose hull would resist the pressure of the ice and could be driven into the frozen sea north of Siberia, it might drift westward across the North Pole to the Atlantic Ocean in about eighteen months—or so he thought.

The Norwegian Parliament accepted to finance the project and Nansen began to think about the construction of a boat with a sturdy, smooth, wooden hull on which the ice could not grip. Designed by the well-known shipwright Colin Archer, *Fram* was launched on 29 October 1892. She was a sailing ship, but her specifications included a steam engine driving a propeller, which, like the rudder, could be retracted so as not to be damaged by the ice. The ship was to be the home of thirteen men for possibly five years and, apart from supplies of dried and concentrated food and different types of fuel, was equipped with everything from bolts of cloth to books and barometers. Significantly, the paraffin "Primus" stove had just been invented and Nansen purchased some. A wind-powered generator supplied electric light. The ship was ready in April 1893 and finally sailed from Christiana on 24 June. Once out to sea, due to her rounded hull *Fram* rolled violently which made Nansen seasick—but, as all seamen know, an uncomfortable ship is a safe ship. After sailing up the west coast of Norway *Fram* headed along the Russian coast to a place called Khabarova where she picked up a large number of sledge dogs and continued to sail east.

Even though it was summertime, they found their route continuously blocked by pack ice, so it was not until 9 September with great jubilation that they rounded Cape Chelyuskin, the northernmost point of continental Siberia, and sailed east across the Laptev Sea. The plan was to go as far north-east as possible before becoming trapped in the winter ice. Finally, on 21 September they were brought to a halt above the 78th parallel and by 5 October the *Fram* could be said to be embedded in the ice. The strong, rounded hull resisted the ice perfectly.

Scurvy, caused by the prolonged lack of fresh food, was still the bane of polar exploration and always fatal. The Vikings had already learned to take berries on long sea voyages, but it was not until 1932—nearly forty years in the future—that the lack of vitamin C was finally identified as the root cause of scurvy. The *Fram* carried quantities of tinned vegetables that were a good source of vitamin C. In his account of the voyage, Nansen mentions special occasions when dried cranberries, blueberries, whortleberries, tinned strawberries, nuts and lime juice were served. Furthermore and quite unknowingly, Nansen had ordered half a ton of cloudberry (similar to a raspberry) jam to be carried on board. Because of these sources of vitamin C there were no cases of scurvy during the three-year voyage.

By October 1894, one year after being trapped in the ice, Nansen realised that the direction of drift was more westward than northward and therefore *Fram* would not approach anywhere near the North Pole. They found themselves over a profound and previously unknown Arctic Ocean—in fact, they discovered that the Arctic consisted of a deep ocean surrounded by land. Nansen now conceived the ambition of making a dash for the pole with one companion using dog sledges. This would take place in the spring, the idea being that the sledging party might be picked up on its return journey by a sealing ship hunting off the archipelago of Franz-Josef Land or Spitsbergen. After two false starts, Nansen and his companion Johansen left the ship in March 1895.

It should be noted that the departure of Nansen had a positive effect on morale. He was not a good leader of men and was considered by his crew as selfish, arrogant and moody. He interfered in everything and insisted on doing things his way. One member of the team noted in his diary at Christmas 1895 that "everything is running more smoothly since Nansen left." Even if he did not make a good leader of men, it is true to say that Nansen inspired this expedition and many of the polar expeditions that followed.

On 15 November 1895, the marooned *Fram* reached its most northerly point—85°55'N. But by the middle of March 1896 she had drifted more than 400 kilometres to the south-west and was obviously moving towards the edge of the ice. On 3 June the ship began to float again, but would not break free of the pack ice for another two months. To force their way through the ice floes they sometimes used explosives. Finally, at 3.45 a.m. on 13 August she sailed out into open water. Sverdrup, the skipper, went first to nearby Spitsbergen to see if there was any news of Nansen—but there was none.

Sverdrup then headed for the Norwegian port of Skjærvø and signalled the arrival of the *Fram* to the world on 20 August 1896 by telegraph. There he learned that Nansen was also safe and would meet him in Tromsø, only about 100 kilometres away. The return of *Fram* and all its crew to Christiana on 9 September was even more triumphal than Nansen's return from Greenland seven years earlier.

THE DASH FOR THE POLE

In his attempt to be the first to reach the North Pole, Nansen proposed to take with him one travelling companion, Hjalmar Johansen. The American explorer Robert Peary had learned to use dogs from the Eskimos for his 1886 expedition and Nansen had learned from Peary. Subsequently, due to his forced stay in Greenland in the winter of 1888/1889, Nansen had understood how to use dog sledges to cross the ice and kayaks for open water—evidently the sledges should be able to carry the kayaks and the kayaks should be able to carry the sledges. The two kayaks could be attached side by side like a catamaran on open water, the sledges lashed on crossways and a sail raised. He had wanted dogs on Greenland as well but did not have the time and opportunity to obtain them. Throughout the long winter night of 1894–1895 experiments were carried out on board the *Fram* on the best type of ski, sledge, kayak, clothing, etc. The Primus stove was tried out at −36°C and found to melt snow into water with spectacular efficiency, so there would be and there was no problem with thirst.

On 26 February 1895 the *Fram* was at the 84th parallel and Nansen decided it was time to set off. There were two false starts due to problems with the weight of the sledges leading to major modifications. Finally, on 14 March the two men actually left for good with three sledges pulled by twenty-eight dogs planning to head north for thirty days. Regrettably, the dogs would be sacrificed one by one as the journey progressed.

The task for Nansen and Johansen was interminable. At the end of each day's run they had to feed the dogs, pitch the silk tent, rearrange the loads on the sledges, carry out running repairs on the dogs' harnesses, check their position, write their diaries and cook the evening meal—all of this in temperatures of –40°C.

Soon after reaching the 85th parallel progress became painfully slow due to numerous pressure ridges of ice blocking their path, together with crevasses filled with seawater, over which the sledges had to be manhandled. Furthermore, they were further hampered by the southward drift of the ice. By 7 April Nansen estimated their position as 86°14'N, the furthest north ever reached, but it was still nearly 400 kilometres to the pole and 600 kilometres south to the nearest land. Exhausted, the following day they decided to turn south.

At first, Nansen and Johansen made tremendous progress because they ran between the pressure ridges instead of across them—then their troubles began. The first and most disastrous problem was that they forgot to wind their watches, both of which stopped. Although they rewound them, from now on plotting their position became a "guesstimate." The further south they travelled the more they found the ice was now drifting north and west, with the danger that they would miss finding land. They had no clear idea of where they would end up. At first they thought they would reach the Franz-Josef Archipelago, then Spitsbergen (modern Svalbard) or even a fictitious Petermannland Archipelago. As the spring advanced the snow conditions deteriorated and they frequently had to make detours around open stretches of water. They realised that they would soon be obliged to launch their kayaks—which had been damaged by sharp edges on the ice. Although their food supplies began to dwindle, seals and polar bears became so plentiful that the two men and their remaining dogs could feast on meat and blubber. From Midsummer's Day 1895 for a whole month they camped on an ice flow making their kayaks seaworthy. On 22 July they set off again on the ice with two lightened sledges carrying the kayaks and pulled by themselves and the last two dogs. The following day they saw land—in fact it had been visible to them for some time, but they failed to realize what it was.

However, actually reaching the land was to prove difficult because the ice across which they were travelling was drifting away from the coast. On 6 August they reached the true edge of the pack ice, which meant the death sentence for the last two dogs. The two men then alternately sailed their "catamaran kayaks" and sledged across the ice towards the land, but it was not until 15 August that they were actually able, with immense relief, to stand on solid ground. Ominously, Nansen noted in his diary that they would probably have to spend yet another winter on this unknown land.

They sailed south along a broken coastline until they realised that the time had come to make a winter camp before it was too late. Finding a sheltered cove with a flat piece of land, on 7 September they began to build a hut with dry stone walls measuring about two metres by three and sunk a metre into the ground. Nansen found a driftwood tree trunk for the roof truss and they covered it in walrus hide. With their guns they had managed to shoot twelve polar bears and four walruses, so they had a more than adequate supply of frozen meat which they cooked on a blubber stove. On 28 September they moved into their new house.

On 15 October the sun disappeared and their third polar night began. Nansen now had plenty of time to establish that their true position was 81°17'N, but since their watches had stopped they had no way of establishing their longitude, so they still did not know whether they were on Franz-Josef Land or Spitsbergen or on some other uncharted archipelago. Due to errors by the early map-makers, they were unable to reconcile the islands around them with what was marked on the maps. During the long winter they patched up their clothes and kayaks and made a new bearskin sleeping bag.

It was not until the beginning of May 1896 that the two filthy soot-grimed savages were ready to continue their journey. They continued southward pulling their shortened sledges over the sea ice experiencing problems with soft snow, attacks by polar bears and walruses, until they were held up for two weeks by storms. On 12 June they reached open sea on what appeared to be the southern coast of the still unknown archipelago. They began to sail westward along the edge of the pack ice, while Nansen became ever more convinced that their true position must be off the southern end of Franz-Jozef Land. At one point, they landed to cook a meal but failed to secure their kayaks, which were carried off by the waves. In desperation, Nansen jumped into the icy sea and swam after them, just managing to reach the boats, crawl into one of them and bring them to the shore—almost dead from exposure.

Then, on 15 June an angry walrus drove its tusks into Nansen's kayak and it started to take on water. In extremis, he reached the edge of the ice before the kayak sank. They were obliged to camp in order to make repairs. Waking up at midday on 17 June, they could hear dogs barking! When Nansen went to investigate, he found that by the most extraordinary chance they had landed near the base camp of a British polar expedition led by F.G. Jackson. Nansen and Jackson knew each other and had each half-expected to meet the other; Jackson was even carrying letters for Nansen!

Jackson's polar expedition was now relegated to the role of Nansen's rescuers. Upon checking their watches with Jackson, they found that they were just 26 minutes slow which had put them 6½° from their true position. It was also discovered that both Nansen and Johansen had gained weight during their long ordeal. Due to the pack ice, it took several weeks for Jackson's supply vessel *Windward* to arrive. Nansen became impatient and even wished that he had pushed on to Spitsbergen, which lay 260 kilometres to the west. It was not until 7 August 1896 that the ship was able to approach the coast and pick up her passengers. Six days later Nansen and Johansen reached the port of Vardø in the extreme north-east of Norway and were able to signal their survival by telegraph to the world.

One week later Nansen met up with Sverdrup and the other members of the crew on board the *Fram* in Tromsø. Once more Nansen had more or less succeeded in his enterprise without any loss of life. With the combination of guns, skis, dogs, sledges and kayaks, he had revolutionized polar travel. Furthermore, neither Nansen nor Johansen nor any member of the crew showed any signs of scurvy. Even though the two men only managed to travel thirty kilometres further north than the drifting *Fram,* this did not diminish their achievement.

NORWAY FINDS A HERO

With his tall, strong build, his blond hair and blue eyes Nansen projected a powerful image to the Norwegian people. At this time Norway existed in a loose union with Sweden and nationalist politicians were looking for a leader: here was one cast in a mighty mould. He was only 35, but respected and esteemed by all his countrymen. Nansen's success as an explorer could be attributed to his self-confidence and physical strength, his ingenuity, his willingness to accept a calculated risk, his thorough planning and attention to detail—it should also be noted that his expeditions were accompanied by a great measure of good fortune! His account of the expedition, *Farthest North,* demonstrated his talent as a writer. The book became an instant best seller.

After a strenuous lecture tour of Europe and the United States, Nansen was made professor of zoology at Christiana University—a post without any duties. He edited the six volumes of the scientific outcomes of the expedition. His research had proved beyond doubt that there was no land close to the North Pole on the Eurasian side, but a deep, ice-covered ocean.

Fourteen years later, a projected expedition to the South Pole could have been the crowning achievement of his scientific career. However, in 1910, Roald Amundsen asked Nansen if he could borrow his ship the *Fram* for a lengthy voyage to the north of Siberia that might yield invaluable oceanic discoveries. Nansen pondered the question, since he had been thinking about his own major expedition, but by now aged nearly 50 he had relinquished all hopes of leading it. With a heavy heart, he decided to hand *Fram* over to Amundsen. In fact, Amundsen's voyage to Siberia was a subterfuge. He had spoken of reaching Siberia by sailing through the Atlantic, Indian and Pacific Oceans and through the Bering Straits, but it seemed odd that when he left

Norway he already had a large team of sledge dogs on board—passing twice through the tropics? Once in mid-Atlantic he changed course and headed for the Antarctic where his team of dog-sledgers would be the first to reach the South Pole. He achieved his goal on 14 December 1911 without a single mishap, beating the British expedition led by Captain Scott by several weeks. Scott and all his companions would die on their return journey from the pole—of, among other things, scurvy! Due to his change of plan, all trust between Nansen and Amundsen evaporated.

Although Amundsen did not lose any of his men in the Antarctic, the expedition did have one notable casualty. Nansen had persuaded Amundsen to take Hjalmar Johansen with him, his former colleague during his Arctic adventure. Johansen had been unable to readjust to everyday life and had turned into an aimless alcoholic and drifter. He was eventually sent home by Amundsen for insubordination. Johansen's plunge into the abyss ended on 4 January 1913 in Christiana, when he shot himself.

While Scott's ill-conceived and ill-fated expedition was foundering in the Antarctic, Nansen spent a week at the Hotel Westminster in Berlin with a tall, dark, attractive Bohemian lady seventeen years his junior—Scott's wife, Kathleen.

As for Amundsen, he would lead other expeditions to the North Pole. Three men already claimed to have reached the North Pole—Cook in 1908, Peary in 1909 and Byrd in 1926—but there were doubts about the reliability of their declarations. In 1925, Amundsen tried to reach the Pole using two aircraft, but did not succeed and he and his team were lucky to survive. In 1926 he was on board the airship *Norge* piloted by the Italian Umberto Nobile which left Spitsbergen on 11 May 1926, crossed the Pole after sixteen hours and reached Alaska two days later. Thus, Amundsen and his colleague Oscar Wisting were the first men to reach both poles. On 18 June 1928 Amundsen would disappear in an aircraft over the Barents Sea while trying to rescue Nobile whose airship had crashed on the Arctic ice.

Meanwhile, from 1908 to 1917 Nansen devoted his time and energy to oceanography, still in its infancy. It is fair to say that he founded physical oceanography. One of his lasting contributions to this field of science is an explanation of how currents form. It had been thought that the polar ice cap drifted westward due to the effect of the wind, but the voyage of the *Fram* had shown that it was more as a result of the Earth's rotation (the Coriolis effect), accentuated by the depth of the water below the ice. Nansen could not explain it mathematically, so he called upon a Swedish physicist, Vagn Walfrid Ekman, to provide the proof. The "Ekman spiral" became a fundamental principal to explain the behaviour of fluids and gases. Nansen also invented a bottle for the collection of water samples from various depths known as the Nansen bottle that is still in use in its more modern form today.

NOTES

1. The content of this section is drawn largely from: Huntford, R. *Nansen: The Explorer as Hero*. London: Abacus, 1997; Nansen, F. *Farthest North*. New York: Skyhorse, 2008; and Nansen, F. *The First Crossing of Greenland*. New York: Longmans, Green, 1895. We have also benefited greatly from the observations of Carl Emil Vogt.

2. The name "Eskimo" is sometimes considered derogatory because it was said to mean "eater of raw meat." The people of Greenland nowadays prefer other names such as "Inuit," meaning "people." The Inuit people of Greenland refer to themselves as "Greenlanders" or "Kalaallit" in their language. However, in the 1880s and 1890s, the term used by Nansen to describe them was "Eskimo" and was certainly not judgemental, so we have used it here.

Chapter Two

Nansen the Diplomat

A NEW ROLE

By the beginning of the twentieth century, a new generation of polar explorers had arrived on the scene, the most famous of whom was the young Roald Amundsen. This implied that Nansen should find a new field for his energies. The step from scientist to explorer had not been a long one, but that to becoming a diplomat was not at all obvious. Although his abilities as a leader of men had been found to be wanting, as an incorruptible political figurehead he was respected and esteemed by all his countrymen.

Although Norway enjoyed considerable sovereignty, it was in a very loose union sharing a king and a foreign policy with Sweden. In the last years of the nineteenth century, Norwegian culture underwent a nationalist revival, while calls for independence added to the rising tension. In 1895 there was nearly war between the two countries and Norway considered itself sufficiently independent to build fortresses along its border with Sweden. In 1905, Nansen entered the fray by writing a series of lively newspaper articles in favour of independence from Sweden. [1]

When the Swedes made demands that were totally unacceptable to the Norwegians, Nansen was hastily dispatched to Berlin and London to promote the Norwegian point of view. Nansen arrived in these centres of power as an itinerant public relations officer for an unofficial cause. In Berlin he was snubbed but in London he was received by the Foreign Secretary, Lord Lansdowne. Nevertheless, both Germany and the United Kingdom hoped that a peaceful solution would be found.

Such was Nansen's standing among the Norwegians that, in the event of independence, he was asked to act as Norway's prime minister. In fact, many people thought that Nansen wanted to become president. In his diary, he made an entry about himself becoming a president but concluded that he would not do it. Finally, he declined all these offers on the grounds that he was "a scientist and explorer" and not a politician.

On 7 June 1905, the Norwegian cabinet resigned and the Swedish King Oscar II did not appoint another one. This was a very shrewd strategy on the part of the Norwegian Government. Since, in their words, King Oscar had been unable to give Norway a new government, he had ceased to be the king of Norway. The Norwegian Parliament took this as a signal that the union had been dissolved. In mid-October a treaty was signed releasing Norway from Swedish rule. The question was now whether Norway should be a monarchy or a republic. If it was to be the former, a likely candidate for king was the Danish Prince Charles whose wife, Princess Maud, was the daughter of the British King Edward VII. It was Nansen who persuaded Prince Charles to accept the Norwegian crown, but Charles would not assume this responsibility until the Norwegian people had been consulted in a referendum. When this took place the royalists achieved 79% of the vote and a few days later Prince Charles arrived in Christiana, assuming the ancient title of King Haakon VII.

Upon the establishment of the Norwegian monarchy, Nansen was appointed ambassador to London, becoming a readily identifiable figure in diplomatic circles. Having presented his credentials in May 1906, he soon became a close personal friend of the British King Edward VII meeting the men—and particularly the women—who pulled the strings of power. Nansen's wife Eva refused to accompany her husband to the United Kingdom saying that she did not wish to uproot herself and the children. In the meantime, Nansen had become romantically entangled with his wife's riding companion, Sigrun Munthe. Finally, Eva joined Nansen in London briefly in the autumn of 1906 and his affair with Sigrun came to an end—for the time being.

By now it was taken for granted that wherever King Edward VII went Nansen would go too. In November 1907 he was at the king's country residence of Sandringham dancing with queens and princesses and playing cards with dukes and duchesses, when he was informed in a succession of telegrams that his wife was seriously ill in Christiana. He immediately left England by ship. By the time he reached Hamburg a telegram was waiting for him saying that Eva had died of pneumonia. She was 49 years old.

Despite Edward VII's efforts to persuade him otherwise, Nansen decided to relinquish his ambassador's post. The king was on a state visit to Norway when Nansen officially presented his letter of recall in May 1908.

His work in the field of diplomacy apparently completed, Nansen planned to devote the rest of his life to his chosen vocation—science. His titular post at Christiana University was now switched from zoology to oceanography.[2]

A TRIP TO RUSSIA AND THE USA

A Norwegian businessman, Jonas Lied, was hoping to open up a trade route into the Siberian hinterland by sending goods up the River Yenesei by light-er. He chartered a steam cargo ship and sailed from Tromsø on 5 August 1913 with a cargo of cement—on board was Nansen. Lied had thought that his enterprise would have a tangible air of credibility if he took the famous explorer along with him—to Nansen it was a holiday. When they reached their destination at the estuary of the Yenesei River, Nansen was taken on board a cutter that took him 2,200 kilometres to Krasnoyarsk on the upper reaches of the river, which also happened to be located on the Trans-Siberian Railway. His Russian hosts then sent him as a VIP by train to the terminus of Vladivostok on the Pacific coast. Returning to Europe by train and car, he reached St Petersburg on 4 November.

As far as the Russians were concerned, it was a public relations exercise to illustrate their investment in the modernization of Siberia where limitless resources were yet to be exploited. For Nansen, this voyage would reveal its significance some years later. He returned to his oceanographic research projects.

The First World War brought an abrupt end to all research and explora-tion for more than four years. Norway remained neutral but encountered serious difficulties when the United States of America, entering the war on 6 April 1917,[3] imposed a blockade on the export of food to Germany and the Central Powers. Unfortunately, this affected Norway too, which was not self-sufficient in grain. Due to his international fame, in June 1917 Nansen was dispatched to Washington as head of a small delegation with plenipotentiary powers to negotiate a solution to the crisis. He arrived in America at the beginning of July and was soon in touch with Herbert Hoover, head of the United States Food Administration. Hoover, a future president, was a su-premely able man. The two men quickly became good friends, which was to prove fruitful in the following years. Nansen also met President Woodrow Wilson.

For more than a year he led the long and often exasperating discussions to secure food for Norway without giving up the country's neutrality. Finally, cutting through the bureaucratic jungle, he took matters into his own hands signing an agreement with the head of the United States War Trade Board, Vance McCormick, giving Norway yearly shipments of essential supplies in return for certain concessions. Nansen returned to Christiana in May 1918, very impressed with Woodrow Wilson's liberal internationalism which would be an inspiration for him in the coming years. He noted that, despite the war, the Americans believed strongly in humanitarian considerations and he was won over to the Allied cause. He was particularly impressed with Herbert Hoover's efforts in providing practical relief and charity under the

"Belgian Relief Commission." Hoover would be a powerful source of inspiration for Nansen's subsequent humanitarian work.

Since their tryst in a Berlin hotel in 1912, Nansen had been bombarding Kathleen Scott with invitations to accompany him on trips, which she refused. Finally, he begged her to marry him. Because of the age difference and because she knew about Sigrun Munthe, once more she refused. Thus it was that on 17 December 1919 that Nansen married Sigrun. Unfortunately, and despite knowing each other for nearly twenty years, it was not always going to be a happy marriage.[4]

NANSEN AND THE LEAGUE OF NATIONS

As he grew older, Nansen became more and more interested in the relations between individuals and nations. The First World War had aroused in him abhorrence for the senseless slaughter of warfare. As soon as he learned of American President Wilson's speech known as the Fourteen Points, Nansen became involved in a Norwegian society supporting the creation of "a general association of nations" and was appointed its chairman. Thus, when the Paris Peace Conference began to talk about a League of Nations to guarantee peace, he was immediately interested. The Big Four—Clemenceau for France, Orlando for Italy, Lloyd George for the United Kingdom and Wilson for the United States—dictated the terms at the Peace Conference in Paris, while the smaller, neutral nations, like Norway, stood on the sidelines. Germany had lost the war and was excluded.

Earlier, on 3 March 1918 Russia had negotiated a separate peace with Germany and the Ottoman Empire at Brest-Litovsk and was now ruled by men who were variously labelled as Communists, Marxists, Soviets or simply Bolsheviks. Throughout the nineteenth century, the United Kingdom and France had opposed Russian access to the Bosporus and the Dardanelles. However, in the spring of 1915 Paris and London agreed that after the war Russia would take possession of them, as well as the city of Constantinople and the adjacent coastal regions, in return for opening an Eastern Front against Germany. The political and military situation had changed so drastically that obviously this was now no longer going to happen, and the isolation of Soviet Russia was a golden opportunity to forget all about it. The Allies were blockading that country in an attempt to influence the political situation. Many people thought that the Bolshevik regime was doomed.

Nansen saw the founding of the League of Nations as a new hope for mankind, but in Paris his only function was that he formed part of a large body of militants, humanitarians and interested parties who might be loosely termed "hangers-on." On his way to Paris, Nansen had visited Kathleen Scott in London. She was on familiar terms with Colonel E.M. House, President

Wilson's closest personal advisor, and she gave Nansen a letter of introduction to hand over to Colonel House at the Peace Conference.

While all relations with Russia had been cut, delegates were aware that there was a severe food shortage in that country. Members of President Wilson's entourage, such as Herbert Hoover and Colonel House, now thought that supplying food to Russia might be another way of influencing the political and military situation. They knew, however, that Lenin would reject outright any direct approach by a Western government due to Allied support for the White Russians in the on-going Civil War. Over dinner on 4 March 1919, the American delegation decided that what was needed was a disinterested proposal to provide food to the Soviet authorities from a respected international figure from a neutral country. The following day Nansen presented his letter of introduction to Colonel House.

Nansen was already familiar to many members of the American delegation, such as Wilson, Hoover and McCormick. Given Nansen's reputation for forthrightness and his naïve desire to intervene in areas of human suffering, McCormick wrote in his diary: "I believe he is the man."[5] Nansen did not seem to realise the complexity of the situation and that he was to be used as a political pawn.[6]

The first move was that on 3 April 1919 Hoover wrote a letter for Nansen's signature addressed to the Big Four in which he posed as an impartial neutral proposing humanitarian aid for the USSR. The following letter was addressed to President Wilson:

> My dear Mr President,
> The present food situation in Russia, where thousands of people are dying monthly from sheer starvation and disease, is one of the problems now uppermost in all men's minds. As it appears that no solution of this food and disease question has so far been reached in any direction I would like to make a suggestion from a neutral point of view for the alleviation of this gigantic misery, on purely humanitarian grounds.
>
> It would appear to me possible to organize a purely humanitarian commission for the provisioning of Russians with the food stuffs and medical supplies to be paid for perhaps to some considerable extent by Russia itself, the justice of distribution to be guaranteed by such a Commission to be comprised of Norwegian, Swedish and possibly Dutch, Danish and Swiss nationalities. It does not appear that the existing authorities in Russia would refuse the intervention of such a commission of a wholly non-political order, devoted solely to the humanitarian purpose of saving life. If thus organized upon the lines of the Belgian Relief Commission, it would raise no question of political recognition or negotiations between the Allies and the existing authorities in Russia.
>
> I recognize keenly the large political issues involved and I would be glad to know under what conditions you would approve such an enterprise and whether such Commission could look for actual support in finance, shipping and food and medical supplies from your Government.

A fortnight later came the reply. It was warm in its approval of Nansen's scheme, and offered all the facilities for carrying out the work—provided all hostilities in Russia ceased. The last condition meant that the scheme was unworkable.

At the same time, the White Armies, under Kolchak in the east of Russia, Denikin and Wrangel in the south and others with the support of the Allies, were attacking the Red Army. When Nansen, after some difficulty, got into touch with Georgy Chicherin, the People's Commissar for Foreign Affairs in the Soviet Government, it was really too late. Opposition had been aroused among the Russian émigrés. What it meant to them and to politicians in some other countries was that feeding the starving Russian people was equivalent to supporting the Bolshevik revolutionary government.

Nevertheless, with the agreement of the Big Four, a carefully worded telegram was sent to Lenin in Moscow on 4 May from the Norwegian Foreign Ministry in Christiana. Lenin saw through Nansen's "humanitarian" gesture to the "political" motives lurking behind it. Prompted by Lenin, Chicherin wrote a long answer to Nansen which contained the following passage:

> If left in peace and allowed free development, Soviet Russia would soon be able to restore her national production, to regain her economic strength, to provide for her own needs and to be helpful to other countries. But in the present situation into which she has been put by the implacable policy of the associated powers, help in foodstuffs from abroad would be most welcome to Russia. The Russian Soviet Government appreciates most thankfully your humane and heartfelt response to her sufferings, and considering the universal respect surrounding your person will be especially glad to enter into communication with you for the realization of your scheme of help which you emphasize as being purely humanitarian.
>
> On this basis of a humanitarian work of help to suffering people we would be pleased to do everything in our powers to further the realization of your project. Unfortunately, your benevolent intentions which you indicate yourself as being based upon purely humanitarian grounds and which, according to your letter must be realized by a commission of fully non-political character, have been mixed up with others with political purposes. In the letter addressed to you by the four Powers your schemes represented as involving cessations of hostilities and of transfer of troops and war materials and we regret very much that your original intentions have been thus fundamentally disfigured by the governments of the associated powers.

Although Nansen thought that he would still be able to help the Russian people, the Big Four knew that they their plan to influence the political situation in Russia had failed. Nansen then proposed to travel to Petrograd (as Saint Petersburg had been known since 1914) to negotiate directly with the Bolsheviks, but Hoover persuaded him otherwise. The whole matter was quietly dropped. Although he lectured in favour of the League of Nations, Nansen's first impression of it was one of disillusion. In his book, *Russia and Peace* (1923), Nansen makes the following comment:

> I am convinced that if these negotiations had attained their object the state of affairs in Europe would have been entirely different from what we see today. The raising of the blockade and Russia's renewed entry into relations with the outside world on a purely economic basis at a time when she still possessed considerable supplies of raw materials would unavoidably have exerted a great influence on the restoration or the equilibrium of European production and consumption.

Despite the fact that the emergency plan to aid the victims of the Russian famine had failed, Nansen made a number of useful contacts in Paris, first and foremost among whom was Philip Noel-Baker,[7] the secretary to Lord Robert Cecil who was himself the head of the League of Nations Section of the British Foreign Office. Noel-Baker was to become a central figure in the Secretariat of the League of Nations and would draw Nansen's attention to the League's potential for humanitarian work.

THE SEQUEL TO THE WAR

By the time the fighting ended in November 1918, the First World War had had a profound impact on Europe and Europeans. Apart from the unprecedented death toll, the psychological and physical damage on people, and the destruction of towns and villages, it had changed social, political and economic systems forever. By the war's end, four major imperial powers—the German, Russian, Austro-Hungarian and Ottoman Empires—had ceased to exist. The successor states of Germany and Russia both lost a great deal of their territory, while the latter two empires disappeared entirely from the map. From the ruins of these empires, a number of smaller states were now created in Central Europe and the Middle East.

Anti-war sentiment had risen across the world. The First World War was described as "the war to end all wars" and its possible origins were vigorously analysed with a view to making sure the same thing would not occur again in future. Among the causes identified were the arms race, political alliances, secret diplomacy, but particularly the autonomy of the rulers of sovereign states to declare war simply on the basis of their own appreciation of the situation. One proposed remedy was for all the nations of the world to become members of an international organization whose aim was to prevent future war through disarmament, open diplomacy, international co-operation, restrictions on the right to wage war, but especially through economic sanctions that would make war unattractive to an aggressor. As a result of the signing of the Treaty of Versailles, the League of Nations was created—the starting point for Nansen's humanitarian career.

It is necessary to distinguish between the Council of the League of Nations, which met nearly every month, and the Assembly, which was an annual event. After his brush with the Big Four during the Paris Peace Conference, Fridtjof Nansen was present with the Norwegian delegation when the first Assembly of the League of Nations met in Geneva on 15 November 1920. With his tall, bony figure, snow-white hair, flowing moustache and broad-brimmed hat set at a rakish angle, he cut an inimitable figure. Nansen was to remain a prominent member of the League until his death in 1930 and was present at the first ten Assemblies between 1920 and 1929.

He was appointed as a member of the Fifth Committee dealing with the admission of new members and to the Sixth Committee on Mandates, Armaments and Economic Weapons. His particular functions on the Fifth Committee were concerned with the Caucasian countries, while for the Sixth Committee he was the Chairman of the Mandates Group. It would be true to say that, in spite of all the time and care Nansen gave to such questions as mandates and disarmament and other important matters, his real influence came through his personality—his goodwill and practical straightforwardness helped to smooth over many a difficulty outside the meetings of the Assembly. Throughout his speeches in the meetings themselves runs the theme of the necessity of getting beyond words to actions and making the League a dynamic and beneficial agent in the world. In one speech he said: "We cannot wait for this international soul to develop of itself. We must do things in order to create it." He was on his guard about anything that would weaken the League's prestige and rejoiced at any achievement that would contribute to improving that prestige. One principle he constantly favoured was that whatever the League undertook must be carried through to successful completion. In the matters for which he was responsible, he spared no efforts to put that principle into effect. He put it this way during one of the League's Assembly meetings: "The wonderful eloquent speech which we have just heard reminds me of the difference between the difficult and the impossible. The difficult is what can be done at once: the impossible is that which takes a little longer."

With the League of Nations as a platform, Nansen became involved in humanitarian work on a grand scale. His struggle for human rights and human values changed diplomats' and politicians' attitudes about their own actions and brought a new dimension to international politics. Nansen gradually became something unique—an international public figure.

SETTING UP THE LEAGUE OF NATIONS

The United States entered the First World War on 6 April 1917 as a direct result of attacks by German submarines on American merchant shipping. Since 1914, President Woodrow Wilson, a democrat, had managed to keep the United States out of the war, but had issued severe warnings to Germany about respecting the freedom of the seas for the merchant ships of neutral nations. Following a change of tactics on the part of the German high command, in the early part of 1917 German submarines began sinking merchant shipping indiscriminately. In a perfectly ruinous move, Germany also promised to help Mexico mount an attack against Texas, which outraged American public opinion. Congress needed little persuasion that the United States should enter the war on the side of the Allies.

While trench warfare was still pursuing its terrible course on the Western Front, a number of governments and groups had already started thinking about a change in international relations so as to prevent another such conflict. One group was led by Woodrow Wilson and his adviser Colonel House, who enthusiastically promoted the idea of a "League of Nations" as a means of avoiding any repetition of the bloodshed. The creation of the League was the last in Wilson's Fourteen Points speech to Congress on 8 January 1918.

In summary, the first thirteen of Wilson's Fourteen Points were as follows:

1. The elimination of secret diplomacy;
2. Freedom of navigation upon the seas;
3. The removal of economic barriers;
4. Limiting armaments;
5. Taking the interests of the people into account in colonial claims;
6. The evacuation of all Russian territory by foreign powers;
7. The restoration of Belgian sovereignty;
8. The return of Alsace-Lorraine to France;
9. The readjustment of the frontiers of Italy along clearly recognized lines of nationality;
10. Autonomous development of the peoples of Austria-Hungary;
11. Free and secure access to the sea for Serbia;
12. The Dardanelles permanently opened as a free passage for shipping;
13. An independent Polish State with secure access to the sea.

The fourteenth point requested the creation of a League of Nations in these words: "A general association of nations must be formed under specific covenants for the purpose of affording mutual guarantees of political independence and territorial integrity to great and small states alike."[8]

After the Allied victory in November 1918, the Paris Peace Conference took place in France from January to June 1919. This conference brought together: Woodrow Wilson for the United States; David Lloyd George for the United Kingdom; Georges Clemenceau for France; and Vittorio Orlando for Italy; as well as some thirty statesmen representing other countries.

During the plenary session of the Conference held on 25 January 1919, the delegates accepted President Wilson's proposal to create a League of Nations. On 28 June, forty-four states signed the Covenant establishing the League of Nations, which actually formed Part I of the Treaty of Versailles. Wilson would be awarded the Nobel Peace Prize in October 1919 for his efforts. The American President had returned to the United States in July and embarked on a nation-wide campaign to secure the support of the American people for their country's entry into the League. Despite his efforts, support was lukewarm. Opposition in the Senate, particularly from Republican politicians Henry Cabot Lodge and William E. Borah, adhered to the nineteenth-century Monroe Doctrine which stated that the Americans would not intervene in European affairs. The United States would never ratify the Covenant of the League of Nations.

SOWING THE SEEDS OF FUTURE PROBLEMS

Some of the most intractable problems of the modern world have roots in the decisions made by the Big Four—France, Italy, the United Kingdom and the United States of America—when preparing the Treaty of Versailles. Among them, one could list the Balkan wars between 1992 and 1999; the crisis of Iraq (whose present borders resulted from Franco-British rivalries and map-making); the continuing quest of the Kurds for self-determination; disputes between Greece and Turkey; and the endless struggle between Jews and Arabs about what each thought they had been promised.

As the peacemakers met in Paris, new nations emerged. Great empires had died or ceased to exist. Particularly, Russia had lost large parts of its territory: the Baltic States, Ukraine, Armenia, Georgia, Azerbaijan and Dagestan were all now ready to declare their independence. Russia itself was under the power of the Bolsheviks and in the middle of a civil war. Lloyd George, as he informed the Supreme Council on 16 January, would have preferred to include Russia in the Peace Conference, but this proved to be an impossible task. The uncertainty and fear of Bolshevism among European countries was a major factor with the result that there was not much support from the other Allies. The Bolsheviks themselves were extremely distrustful of outside interference in their affairs and showed no enthusiasm to participate. Furthermore, with the Civil War taking place in Russia, the Big Four were not in a position to say who really represented the country, and therefore they were unable to reach any decision on the matter.[9]

The Allied Powers had set up an ambitious programme for the Conference with the hope of re-organizing the world. However, the problems they encountered were far more complex than they could ever have anticipated. The aftermath of the war gave rise to the Russian revolution, severe unemployment and a flood of refugees. Facing domestic pressure, events they could not control and conflicting claims they could not reconcile, the negotiators were in the end simply overwhelmed—and made quick deals and compromises that would echo down throughout the history of the twentieth century.[10] Their task was made more difficult by the passage of time. As the months went by and their military forces dispersed, the Big Four were less able to impose their will.

In Versailles heads of state, their experts and delegations were assigned to commissions, which held more than 1,000 sessions to prepare reports on topics ranging from prisoners of war, undersea telephone cables, trade and international aviation, and inevitably to whom was responsible for the war. Wilson was convinced that there was something profoundly wrong when millions of people were slaughtered in an apparently pointless conflict. He was particularly critical of old-fashioned European diplomacy whose treaties obliged countries to go to war with their otherwise peaceful neighbours and where governments made no effort to consult their people before taking momentous decisions affecting the fate of mankind. He put it this way: "It was a war determined upon as wars used to be determined upon in the old, unhappy days when peoples were nowhere consulted by their rulers and wars were provoked and waged in the interest of dynasties or of little groups of ambitious men who were accustomed to use their fellow men as pawns and tools." It followed that key recommendations were included into the Treaty of Versailles with Germany, which had fifteen chapters and 440 clauses. After six months of tremendously hard work, the major outcome of the Peace Conference was the creation of the League of Nations and the Treaty of Versailles between the Allies and Germany.

But there were treaties for the other defeated nations as well—the Treaty of Saint-Germain with Austria, the Treaty of Neuilly with Bulgaria, the Treaty of Trianon with Hungary and the Treaty of Sèvres with the Ottoman Empire. On 10 August 1920, representatives of Mehmet VI, the last Ottoman Sultan, signed the Treaty of Sèvres. Events in Turkey had, however, moved with startling rapidity. A new government, the Turkish Grand National Assembly, under the leadership of Mustafa Kemal (Atatürk) was formed on 23 April 1920 in Ankara. Turkish nationalists rejected the settlement by the Sultan's four signatories with the result that by 1923 the peace had to be renegotiated—the Treaty of Lausanne with the newly formed Republic of Turkey.

The five major powers (France, Italy, Japan, the United Kingdom and the United States) controlled the Peace Conference. In practice, Japan played a minor role. Eventually, to speed matters along, the Big Four met together informally and made all the major decisions, which in turn were ratified by the other nations during plenary meetings.

As Margaret MacMillan points out in her book *Paris 1919*, the peacemakers attempted to resolve all of the world's problems, but even they sensed that they were in fact laying the seeds for future turmoil. "I cannot say for how many years, perhaps I should say for how many centuries, the crisis which has begun will continue," predicted Georges Clemenceau, whose own behaviour contributed to the impending problems. "Yes, this treaty will bring us burdens, troubles, miseries, difficulties that will continue for long years."

Although the countries that signed the Covenant of the League of Nations agreed to openness and transparency in diplomacy, in fact the old habits of secrecy and concealment quickly re-established themselves and would soon render the organization futile. However, for the first time it did provide a platform for the smaller nations to express opinions about the policies of their larger neighbours.

All of these problems were secondary to what happened in Germany. The Armistice of 1918 had not been a decisive Allied victory and Germany would react to its defeat in the coming years. The Treaty of Versailles was viewed by some German nationalists as a humiliation that must be avenged, and their attention focused on Part I—the setting up of the League of Nations. Particularly, the Covenant of the League of Nations as an integral part of the Treaty would turn out to be a mistake since the Germans were looking for a focus for their resentment—and here was one ready-made. Who or what was it that had actually caused the German downfall? In identifying another scapegoat attention turned on the Jewish element of the population who, it was believed by extremist elements, had poisoned the wellsprings of pure German culture. Anti-Semitism erupted into violence on 24 June 1922 with the assassination of the German Foreign Minister Walther Rathenau, an international Jewish figure—as also was Albert Einstein. Rathenau's murderers, two right-wing army officers, were hunted down and shot. Later, in 1929 with the Stock Market Collapse the ground was ready for political extremism to surface. In January 1933 Adolf Hitler came to power and one of his first acts was the public honouring of Rathenau's murderers. Then his attention turned to the complete humiliation of the next victim: the League of Nations. All of this was the prelude to another arms race and the Second World War.

Between January and June 1919 the peacemakers had accomplished an enormous amount: the founding of the League of Nations and the International Labour Organisation; mandates handed out on the government of Germany's and the Ottoman Empire's former territories; the German treaty finished; the treaties with Austria, Hungary and Bulgaria nearly done—but there were many loose ends. Russia's borders were still fluctuating, while the proposed treaty with Ottoman Turkey collapsed. In Europe the borders were still being disputed and it was not clear which states would keep their new independence. What was happening about Finland? Ukraine? Georgia? Armenia? The Kurds? And the decision taken so lightly to let the Greeks take possession of Smyrna (modern Izmir in Turkey) had set off a disastrous chain reaction that would not end until 1923, generating a huge number of refugees.

Moreover, some of the great problems that had faced the peacemakers at the start of the Peace Conference had merely been shelved. Russian Bolshevism had been contained, perhaps, but the long-term European Cold War between the capitalist West and the communist East was only just beginning. The German question was still there to trouble Europe.[11]

Nationalism, far from burning itself out, was still gathering momentum. There was much fuel to hand in Central Europe and further afield in the Middle East and in Asia. In many cases the peacemakers found themselves dealing with *faits accomplis*. Yugoslavia, Poland and Czechoslovakia all existed before the Peace Conference started. The best the peacemakers could do was to try to prevent the fragmentation of Europe and the Middle East into further and further subdivisions based on nationality and to draw borders as sensibly as possible. The demand for nation-states based on single nationalities with fixed borders was not entirely rational in the world of 1919. For the next ten years, Nansen would be involved in resolving the unforeseen consequences of the Treaty of Versailles.

NOTES

1. Nansen, F. *Nansens røst: artikler og taler/av Fridtjof Nansen, 1884–1905.* Oslo: Jacob Dybwads Forlag, 1942. (Edited by A.H. Winsnes.) For more information on Norwegian history, information can be found on Store Norske Leksikon.

2. Sorensen, J. *The Saga of Fridtjof Nansen.* London: Allen & Unwin, 1932.

3. As soon as American ships began to be the victim of this new German policy, President Wilson outlined the case for declaring war upon Germany in a speech to the joint houses of Congress on 2 April 1917, from which the following paragraph is taken:

With a profound sense of the solemn and even tragical [sic] character of the step I am taking and of the grave responsibilities which it involves, but in unhesitating obedience to what I deem my constitutional duty, I advise that the Congress declare the recent course of the Imperial German Government to be in fact nothing less than war against the government and people of the United States; that it formally accept the status of belligerent which has thus been thrust upon it; and that it take immediate steps not only to put the country in a more thorough state of defence but also to exert all its power and employ all its resources to bring the Government of the German Empire to terms and end the war.

A formal declaration of war followed four days later. (President Wilson's Declaration of War Message to Congress, 2 April 1917. *Records of the United States Senate; Record Group 46.* Washington, DC: National Archives.)

4. Huntford, R. *Nansen: The Explorer as hero,* p. 598. London: Abacus, 1997.

5. Huntford, p. 592.

6. Sorensen, pp. 288–289.

7. In June 1915 Philip Baker married Irene Noel, a field hospital nurse, and in 1923 changed his name to Noel-Baker. Since, throughout his subsequent political career, he was known as Noel-Baker, we have used it here.

8. President Wilson's Message to Congress, 8 January 1918. *Records of the United States Senate; Record Group 46.* Washington, DC: National Archives.

9. United States of America Department of State. *Foreign Relations of the United States, Paris Peace Conference 1919*, volume III, p. 581. Washington, DC: Government Printing Office, 1943.

10. MacMillan, M. *Paris 1919: Six Months that Changed the World,* pp. 18–63. New York, NY: Random House, 2002.

11. Fosse, M.; Fox, J. *The League of Nations: From Collective Security to Global Rearmament.* New York, NY: United Nations, 2012.

Chapter Three

The Prisoners-of-War in Siberia

GETTING TO GRIPS WITH THE PROBLEM

In the month of June 1919, Sir Eric Drummond, the new Secretary-General of the League of Nations, presented a note on the functioning of the future administrative services, of which the Secretariat would initially be installed at Sunderland House in London. There was much to deal with: the permanent location of the seat of the League; the status of the Free City of Danzig; the admission of new member States; the fate of minorities in Turkey. But one issue demanded immediate attention: the plight of prisoners-of-war held in Russia and Siberia.

Estimates of the total number of prisoners-of-war taken during the First World War vary. Figures of between 6 and 8 million have been mentioned, but by 1920 the vast majority of them had managed to find their way home in one way or another. The International Committee of the Red Cross (ICRC) had reported that there were still at least 200,000 prisoners-of-war in Siberia belonging to Germany and various other nationalities of the former Austro-Hungarian Empire: Austrians, Czechs, Slovaks, Hungarians and Romanians. The Swedish Red Cross had made public opinion in Western Europe aware of the circumstances in which these men were being held: many of them had been captured in 1914 and were now facing their sixth Siberian winter living in inadequately heated and overcrowded quarters, lying on bare boards wearing the rags of uniforms they had worn since they were captured. Their food was quite inadequate and they had no money to pay for the bare necessities of life. Technically, the Bolsheviks had released the prisoners and they were free to go wherever they pleased—but the transport system had collapsed. Locked in the grip of a Civil War, the Russians were largely indifferent to their fate. If these men were not returned home before the winter of 1921, they were likely to die of hunger, cold and neglect.[1]

By 27 September 1919 the Supreme Economic Council of the League of Nations had become aware of their situation and proposed setting up a repatriation commission.[2]

In January 1920, the Secretary-General of the League received the unofficial visit of representatives from the Society of Friends' Emergency and War Victims Relief Committee, who had gathered information from more or less reliable sources showing that there still remained some 400,000 prisoners held in Russia.[3] Of these, 100,000 were located east of Lake Baikal. Furthermore, the British High Commissioner at Irkutsk had estimated that at the beginning of December 1919 there were 50,000 Austrians and 10,000 German prisoners-of-war in places not under the control of the Soviet Government. There were also some former Turkish and Bulgarian soldiers held in Russian camps. To these figures should be added huge numbers of prisoners-of-war of the former Tsarist Russia held in Germany and not yet repatriated. Finally, a small number of Allied prisoners had been captured by the Bolsheviks during military operations in support of the White Russians. Since the Allies did not recognize the Soviet Government and wanted this state-of-affairs to continue, they were keen for the League of Nations to act as an intermediary in bringing these men home. This was also a way of sharing the cost among several countries.

Amid growing concern, the Red Cross had been approached by the German Government about the exchange of Russian prisoners in Germany for German prisoners in European Russia and Siberia. A limited prisoner exchange programme had been going on between Russia and Germany since March 1918, but required considerable co-ordination with Poland and the Baltic countries—not to mention the Allies. The German office responsible for prisoner-of-war issues was under the responsibility of the enterprising Social Democrat Moritz Schlesinger.

Millions of Europeans still had relatives in captivity and for them the war was not over. The Allied military authorities had a repatriation scheme that began functioning in January 1919 mainly under the responsibility of the Germans, but the Allies refused to pay for it, while many countries of Eastern and Central Europe could not afford to repatriate their own countrymen. Another reason for the Allies to show a lack of enthusiasm was that prisoners-of-war repatriated from Germany to Russia could easily be used to strengthen Bolshevik military forces fighting the White Russians. Even so, some Russians were being used by the German military to oppose the Bolsheviks in East Prussia. Meanwhile, in the prisoner-of-war camps there was conflict between White Russian and Bolshevik agitators who tried to set off uprisings among the prisoners, which could easily have led to de-stabilizing Germany itself. Germany was considered vulnerable to chaos due to communist revolutionary and counter-revolutionary movements.

The United States, under the direction of Herbert Hoover, was providing extensive aid programmes to the Russian prisoners in Germany. Both President Wilson and Hoover saw the provision of food as a way of bringing stability to Europe and thus halting communism. Nevertheless, most of the prisoners-of-war simply wanted to go home and the Allies were faced with the moral responsibility of doing so for humanitarian reasons. In February 1920, the Allies estimated that all of their own combatants who had been taken prisoner had now been released and therefore removed all further obstacles standing in the way of the repatriation of prisoners of other nations. Now, some kind of supra-national co-ordination was required.

The Allied Economic Commission in Paris recommended that the League of Nations should take responsibility for keeping the prisoners alive and sending them home.[4] The Society of Friends made a proposal to the Secretary-General via the Hungarian Red Cross that a series of rest camps should be created from Siberia to Central Europe so that these men could be brought back in stages. Secretary-General Drummond referred the deputation to the League of Red Cross Societies in Geneva, which he considered as the competent organization to take charge of the matter. He advised them to present the idea to Lieutenant-General Sir David Henderson, its Director, and added that if the latter thought it necessary he would present the case before the Council of the League of Nations. A telegram was sent to Sir David Henderson from Lord Robert Cecil requesting him to present the matter to the monthly meeting of the Council of the League of Nations in February 1920 in Paris.[5]

Secretary-General Drummond was not convinced that the repatriation of prisoners-of-war was actually a matter that should be dealt with by the League of Nations, believing that it was not mandated to intervene. On the other hand, subordinates like Philip Noel-Baker pressed the League to seize this opportunity. In view of the urgent situation, Léon Bourgeois, who was the President of the Council, agreed to include the subject on the provisional agenda of the Council's next meeting.

Thus, at the second session of the Council meeting on the 11 February, the chairman Léon Bourgeois handed to the Council the letter he had received from the Supreme Economic Council and a letter mentioning the Red Cross in Geneva which offered to take charge of repatriation of the prisoners in Siberia—if the Council should request it to do so.[6] It was suggested that the matter should be referred to the Secretary-General of the League for consideration and a report presented at the next meeting of the Council. Apart from setting up this committee to make a report, this game of "pass the parcel" continued during February and March 1920.

In a memorandum to his staff on 16 February Drummond wrote:[7]

The Question of Prisoners-of-war in Russia. Monsieur Bourgeois, at the last meeting of the Council formally placed on the table a Resolution from the Supreme Economic Court dealing with the question. . . . As Dr Nitobe and Dame Rachel Crowdy will before long be going to Geneva to take part in the First General Council of the League of Red Cross Societies, I have asked them to take charge of this question and to prepare the necessary documents for the Council. Meanwhile, I should be glad if . . . Mr Baker will write to Sir David Henderson suggesting to him that a memorandum should be got ready for communication to Dr Nitobe and Dame Rachel Crowdy. [8]

In the letter Drummond's assistant Philip Noel-Baker wrote to Sir David Henderson we read the following:

The whole question of the Prisoners-of-war in Russia and their desperate condition has been brought officially before the Council of the League of Nations by a motion of the Supreme Economic Council. It will therefore come up for consideration at the next meeting of the Council. . . . It is possible, however, that there may be an earlier meeting of the Council held in London, in which case this subject, which is an urgent one, would no doubt be considered. It is quite probable that the Council when it deals with the matter will invite the League of Red Cross Societies to undertake some duties in connection with it. In anticipation that this may occur, and that he may be as fully informed as possible on the whole subject, the Secretary-General has asked Dame Rachel Crowdy of the secretariat and Dr Nitobe . . . to discuss the whole subject with you as fully as possible. He asked me further to suggest to you that it would be very useful if you could prepare for them a memorandum on the present situation including whatever details you may have to the present condition of prisoners, the measures of relief which you consider it would be possible to carry out, points on which you would require authority or assistance from the League and any other general conditions connected with transport, finances or the organisation of relief, which you may think it well to include. [9]

In the meantime, Crowdy and Nitobe, the two senior staff members of the League of Nations mentioned by both Drummond and Noel-Baker, wrote a report on the situation in Siberia. [10] This document—several pages long— gave a complete picture of what the prisoners were enduring. The staff of the League of Nations had already identified that the plan of action for repatriation could be broken down into three parts: (a) preliminary negotiations; (b) the provision of funds; and (c) actually bringing the men home. No satisfactory negotiations could be carried out unless a specific body was appointed and given full power to investigate and negotiate. It should consist of a commissioner appointed by the League of Nations (and given full power by the League), representatives of the Red Cross, the League of the Red Cross Societies, the former warring countries, etc.

This internal report was discussed in the director's meeting on the 31 March 1920, and Secretary-General Drummond suggested that the Council of the League of Nations should appoint one person to determine the true facts, find the necessary money and report to the Council. This person should be advised that much private and a certain amount of governmental effort was being undertaken and it was his task to co-ordinate it all. [11] Thus, finally, at the fourth session of the Council (Paris, 9–11 April 1920), the repatriation of prisoners-of-war in Siberia was at the top of the agenda. At the end of the meeting, the delegates agreed that the task of repatriation should be given "to a person enjoying a world-wide reputation for his organizational and executive abilities and for his high moral standing." What was required was a well-known person from a small neutral country. They already had in mind such a person who had all the qualities needed and who could assume this "heavy but honourable duty."

NANSEN AS HIGH COMMISSIONER

The name of Fridtjof Nansen as a candidate for the position of the High Commissioner of the League of Nations for the Repatriation of Prisoners-of-War was circulating in private correspondence well before his appointment. In fact, on 22 March 1920, just a couple of days after the Secretary-General received the report on the situation of the prisoners-of-war, and before it was circulated to the members of the Council, the name of Nansen appears in correspondence between Noel-Baker of the League and J.A Salter, secretary of the War Reparations Commission based in Paris. Noel-Baker wrote: "the Secretary General believes that if a Commissioner of authority is appointed (such as Dr Nansen) and if this Commissioner set forth the condition of the prisoners and proposing the division of responsibility for the credits in accordance with the plan suggested, then no government would be able to refuse to bear its share, viewing the pressure of public opinion." [12] Salter replied a couple of days later: "I think Dr Nansen would be exactly the person to be in charge." [13]

The Council of the League of Nations decided to telegraph Nansen inviting him to undertake the task of High Commissioner. The outline of a letter was drafted by the Italian delegate. [14]

> Sir,
> The Council of the League of Nations has had under consideration the question of prisoners-of-war now in Siberia, and has instructed me to invite you to investigate on its behalf the problems connected with the repatriation of prisoners-of-war who have not yet been able to return to their homes.
> The Council realizes that, in extending to you this invitation, it is asking you to undertake an arduous and difficult task; but it feels that this work is of real humanitarian importance and of the utmost urgency.
> The Council knows the interest you take in the fate of prisoners, and the great efforts which you and many of your countrymen have made to mitigate

the sufferings caused by the late war. It has therefore every confidence that you will accept the invitation.

The Council recognizes that to carry out the task satisfactorily it will be necessary for you to get in communication, not only with the various voluntary agencies at present helping to ease the suffering of the prisoners, but also with the Governments of all those states concerned directly or indirectly in their repatriation. The Council has therefore instructed me to help you in every way in my power, both in regard to diplomatic and other facilities and in regard to your dealings with the Governments. Should you find it necessary for the execution of your duties to have the services of a small expert secretariat, the Secretary-General will be happy to render you such assistance in its formation as may be in his power, and all the charges and expenses of yourself and staff will be regarded by the Council as charges upon the League.

On the same day—9 April 1920—a telegram almost identical to the draft letter was sent by Sir Eric Drummond to Nansen. Drummond asked to receive a reply by the following day, but Nansen did not reply until 14 April. Furthermore, his reply was communicated by the French Embassy in Christiana, which must have contributed to the delay. When the Council meeting completed its work on 11 April Nansen had not replied and no other name had been put forward, which suggests that the delegates were very keen that Nansen should accept this post. Here is Nansen's reply: [15]

> I am deeply honoured by the confidence that the Council of the League of Nations has shown to me by the proposal of your telegram. It placed me in a very difficult position as the proposition is entirely new to me that I do not know what to answer. I do not grasp how much work it actually would involve, par example whether it would necessitate journeys for examinations of the conditions and numbers of prisoners in Russia, Siberia, etc. As I understand it, not knowing more than your telegram, such a thorough investigation would be required and the whole task would mean years of work in which time one could do nothing else, in that sense I cannot accept this important assignment as it would mean that I had to give up my scientific work. But if I am mistaken, and it means less work than I expect, I might of course reconsider it.

The very same day Sir Eric Drummond replied mellifluously by telegram. [16]

> I have received your telegram. I do not think the work required will be as great as you suppose. It is almost essential that arrangements should be made before next winter for early repatriation of greater part of prisoners, but this having been done; actual execution of measures decided on might be placed in other hands if you personally found it impossible to continue. It is true that for the next few months any other work would no doubt be difficult if not impossible and the investigations are likely to necessitate journeys in Europe and Russia. Nevertheless, the Council would wish me to urge you very strongly to accept their invitations as they could find no one with such great experience and authority to carry out the negotiations [...]. Memorandum follows by post and

if necessary I could send a member of my secretariat to Christiana to explain matters further.

NANSEN ACCEPTS

The original idea was that a "commissioner" would be appointed by the Council of the League of Nations and sent to Russia as the head of a delegation consisting of representatives of the former enemy countries, the Red Cross and some neutral countries—Denmark and Sweden are specifically mentioned in correspondence. In a briefing report prepared by Noel-Baker, Drummond recalled the relationships that Nansen may have established during his voyage to Siberia in 1913. Drummond added: "But all these routes [through Estonia, Poland or the Black Sea] in the last resort depend on the goodwill of the Bolsheviks and on the railway material of which they dispose. I'm sure that in this respect your efforts may be of the greatest value, as the Bolsheviks are well disposed towards you."

Why was Nansen the ideal candidate? He was well-known and trusted by Allied politicians, particularly the British Government and Herbert Hoover. The role of commissioner was a temporary position that did not involve a great deal of power and prestige, only requiring that the job should be done. It was believed that Nansen was viewed sympathetically by the Soviet authorities. He was a legend, a hero, a man who made an instant impression. It may further be pointed out that the League did not have a budget for this operation and it was therefore necessary to appoint a person of private wealth who would be reimbursed for expenses but would not require a salary.

In the exchange of telegrams that followed Nansen said that he was willing to take up the position if he could work out of Christiana. He was in fact feeling restless and was looking for another great adventure. On the 20 April Drummond was anxious to complete the deal and wrote: "I have now heard informally from the President of the Council that he agrees with your proposals. Mr Philip [Noel-]Baker, the official who has been dealing with the subject, left this morning for Christiana and will probably call you on Friday 23 April."[17]

In a letter from Drummond to Léon Bourgeois, chairman of the Council, on the 19 April, we read the following (in French): "As Dr Nansen is the most eminent person qualified for the mission, I believe therefore that we must do everything in our power to ensure his collaboration. Once he has begun his inquiries, I am convinced that he will devote himself body and soul to the success of this task."[18] In a telegram to Drummond, Bourgeois confirmed that he was "absolument d'accord" [entirely in agreement].[19]

When Noel-Baker arrived in Christiana he telephoned Nansen in order to find out how to reach his house. But, much to Noel-Baker's surprise, Nansen, who had returned from the United States in 1918 with a Model "T" Ford, immediately drove himself down to the British Legation.[20] For Noel-Baker and Nansen it was the beginning of a long collaboration, with the latter very quickly agreeing to Drummond's proposal. Some years later, Philip Noel-Baker described their meeting as follows:

> And then for seven hours without one moment's intermission—right through the Minister's luncheon party, through his tea party, till darkness had fallen outside—Nansen asked me questions about how the repatriations could be done. The Legation Chancery had to find him maps; the encyclopaedia had to be consulted; every possible hypothesis and every plan had to be considered and discussed.[21]

It was, indeed, a great meeting of minds: Noel-Baker admired Nansen's international approach, his courage and his impatience with bureaucracy; in Noel-Baker Nansen found an enthusiastic, level-headed and enterprising emissary. Apart from a distinguished academic career, Philip Noel-Baker was a skier and athlete, which appealed to Nansen. He had participated in the 1912 Olympic Games in Stockholm.[22] He was also a Quaker and had served as a non-combatant volunteer in an ambulance unit during the First World War, being decorated for bravery by the British, French and Italians. His influence at the Paris Peace Conference and in the League of Nations was out of all proportion to his junior position and, as far as Nansen is concerned, he emerges time and time again as a key player. Up until 1924, Noel-Baker became Nansen's right-hand man and wrote many of his speeches—even after this date.

On 1 May 1920 Nansen wrote to Torsten Valdemar Lundell at the Swedish Red Cross that he had accepted the job as High Commissioner "in much doubt." There are a number of reasons why he accepted this post but, most of all, he felt a significant moral commitment to humanitarian work. Later he wrote to Lord Robert Cecil that the work he was involved in was "of the greatest humanitarian and political importance." He felt sympathetic towards the Russians and he was keen to play a significant role in the success of the League of Nations. As we have seen, after his visit to the United States in 1917 he had acquired a taste for international humanitarianism.

GETTING THE PRISONERS HOME

Once he had accepted the new assignment, Nansen set to work immediately. If as many prisoners-of-war as possible were to be repatriated before the winter of 1920, it was necessary to start the process already in the spring of that year.

First, Nansen thought it would be very desirable that the League should express its appreciation and gratitude to the Governments of Finland and

Estonia for their help in facilitating the return of prisoners. This would encourage them to continue providing assistance. He also asked the Council of the League to pass a general resolution requesting that prisoners-of-war should be allowed free transit and reasonable medical supervision while passing through third countries on their way home, such as Romania, Ukraine and Poland. In his opinion, it was premature to send clothing, medicine and other supplies for the prisoners, when the whole Siberian population were suffering from the same shortages. Nansen also saw the International Committee of the Red Cross as the key to the success of the enterprise. [23]

Since the end of the First World War, the Allied governments had been deliberately blocking the return of German and Austro-Hungarian prisoners-of-war held in Siberia and of Russian prisoners in German camps until all of their own nationals were returned home. However, in January 1920 the British Government withdrew its objections and the Prime Minister told Parliament that they would now support the actions of the League of Nations. The League acknowledged that the French and Italian Governments also shared the same opinion.

Several non-governmental organizations were already playing a central role in repatriating the prisoners-of-war. The Red Cross, particularly the Swedish and Danish sections, had been concerned with prisoners throughout the First World War and continued to do so during the Russian Civil War. The Red Cross had negotiated an agreement between Germany and the USSR over prisoners-of-war in April 1920 and then managed to extend it to cover all the nationalities concerned. It was therefore in a position to provide expertise. Among other important charitable organizations playing a supporting role was the American Young Men's Christian Association (YMCA).

While the Red Cross had established a system for bringing the prisoners home, it needed money, the consent of the transit countries and the Allies to actually implement it. Shipping was a key issue—the British controlled all German shipping on the Baltic Sea.

The Allied governments did not recognize the Soviet Government, therefore they needed the League of Nations to act as the middleman and the League needed an individual whom the Soviets would accept as an interlocutor. It was evident that the Soviets would recall sympathetically Nansen's efforts in the spring of 1919 to send food aid to Russia. Neither the Soviet nor German Governments were actually consulted as to whether they would accept Nansen as a commissioner. At the beginning of May 1920 Noel-Baker simply informed the Germans and Soviets that the repatriation of prisoners would take place more rapidly if they would provide all the relevant information to Nansen.

WHERE WERE THE PRISONERS LOCATED?

In the first instance, it was impossible to determine the number and residence of prisoners in European Russia, Siberia and Turkmenistan, particularly since many of them were on the move. At this stage and for the same reason, it was also too soon to establish complete plans for their repatriation or estimate the total cost. A group of prisoners had just been repatriated via Narva on the Russian-Estonian frontier to Swinemunde (at that time in Germany, now Świnoujście in Poland). While every effort was being made to consolidate and expand the route through Russia to Estonia, it was also of the greatest importance to open up new routes so that as many prisoners as possible could benefit.

In the spring of 1920, the Red Army invaded Poland. It reached the gates of Warsaw but, to everyone's surprise, the Polish Army then won a decisive battle and drove the Russians out again. This was the context in which the repatriation of prisoners was to take place because it meant that the possibility of returning the prisoners-of-war by land routes across Poland was virtually impossible.

Nansen reported to Sir Eric Drummond that he would be meeting in Berlin with the German Government, the Red Cross and delegates from Austria and Hungary. During this meeting that took place on 18 May Nansen learned that the central German organization for repatriating prisoners and the Red Cross had already reached agreement with the Soviets about the exchange of prisoners before Nansen and the League entered the stage.[24] However, the Red Cross needed political support and money to carry out the plan, and it was anticipated that Nansen and the League would provide both of these. At this meeting a plan of action was adopted and tasks distributed; food and clothing would be supplied; medical posts would be set up on both sides. During the summer of 1920 four ships travelled backwards and forwards across the Baltic ferrying prisoners-of-war in both directions, but it was obvious that their capacity was too limited.[25]

From those who had already returned Nansen had obtained some information about the prisoners-of-war located in Siberia and Turkmenistan. There was the possibility of a route back to Europe from Tashkent to Batum in Georgia, which involved crossing the Caspian Sea to Baku in Azerbaijan. Many prisoners-of-war had set off on this route and had apparently reached Bukhara in Uzbekistan but could not proceed any further. Even if they could reach Krasnovodsk and cross the Caspian Sea, they would have to travel by rail through the Caucasus where fighting was still taking place. In the end, this route was abandoned.

Nansen believed that the prisoners stuck in Turkmenistan were of their own accord actually moving north-west in fairly large numbers along the Russian railway line towards Samara on the Volga River. On the very same day that the Conference opened in Berlin, the League of Nation received an urgent telegram for the Red Cross stating that Ukraine had sent 20,000 prisoners by train to Poland which was threatening to close its border.[26]

Once back in Christiana on 25 May Nansen started work on a plan to repatriate prisoners from Central Russia through the Estonian port of Narva.[27]

Another meeting took place on 16 June at 10 Downing Street in London with members of the British Government and Leonid Krasin, the Soviet Government's representative in London. Nansen was invited to attend since the matter of repatriation was on the agenda.

On 26 June Nansen met Maxim Litvinov, representative of the Soviet Government, and delegates of the Russian Red Cross in Copenhagen. Both the Allies and the Soviets accepted Nansen as playing a role of some importance in Western/Soviet relations because both parties needed a neutral go-between. Internal Soviet correspondence of the time refers to him as "a naïve leftist intellectual" who could easily be exploited.

The discussions in Copenhagen concerned, among other things, the opening up of as many repatriation routes as possible through Latvia and Lithuania. Following this meeting, Nansen decided that it would be profitable to visit Moscow. He travelled alone by sea and by train via Tallinn in Estonia and met Georgy Chicherin, the Soviet Foreign Minister, in Moscow.

As an opening barrage, Chicherin rejected Nansen's credentials from the League of Nations, so Nansen asked at once to be returned to the frontier by special train. Chicherin then backed down and accepted to deal with Nansen as an individual.[28] He introduced him to Alexander Eiduk, who was in charge of the transportation of prisoners of war through an organization called Centroevak. Although Eiduk was a hard-liner and a most unsavoury character, he agreed to bring the prisoners to the border and did indeed respect his part of the deal with Nansen. The Soviets would not allow many foreigners on their territory, including the staff of the Red Cross, but were meticulous in distributing supplies earmarked for prisoners-of-war.

The Soviets declared that they would be able to send one train daily from Moscow to Narva, and perhaps another one to Björkö in Finland where the prisoners could then travel by ship to Swinemunde or Stettin. They also stated that they would run Red Cross trains between Central Russia and Siberia concentrating the prisoners on Moscow. Nansen hoped that 60,000 prisoners would be repatriated before the onset of winter. This route was already functioning and prisoners were arriving rapidly, so rapidly in fact that the Red Cross reported that the Narva Camp was soon overflowing while trains continued to arrive. Narva had become a bottleneck and it was therefore urgent to arrange more maritime transport to avoid the system breaking down. The fact that the prisoners were no longer in Russia but in Estonia meant that the Western leaders could no longer ignore them by saying that they were a Soviet responsibility.

Nansen decided to tackle the British Government about shipping. In fact, the British had impounded the German merchant fleet after the war and it was on these vessels that he had his eye. They were still manned by their German crews and could rapidly be deployed.

It should be pointed out that there were also hundreds of thousands of Russian prisoners-of-war in German camps. The ships bringing the prisoners home from Russia could then take the Russian prisoners back across the Baltic Sea in the other direction. Thus, the final total of men returned home includes not only Western Europeans held in Russia, but also Russians in German prisoner-of-war camps (i.e. soldiers of the former Tsarist Russia).

FINANCIAL MATTERS

Nansen presented a report to the Council of the League of Nations in which he stated that, apart from political problems preventing the repatriation of prisoners, there were three fundamental difficulties:

1. The collapse of government, and especially of means of communication, in many of the territories where the prisoners were located.
2. The complete severance of communication between Russia and the rest of the world.
3. The inability of some of the governments to pay for the cost of transport for their own subjects.

In fact, Austria, Czechoslovakia, Hungary, Poland, Romania and Yugoslavia were unable to pay for the repatriation of their own men. The only realistic option was to grant them international loans to finance transport costs.[29]

On 10 June 1920 Nansen had a meeting in London with Sir William Goode, the British Representative to the Supreme Economic Council,[30] and Sir Eric Drummond and his staff. The meeting was intended to be concerned with the immediate charting of ships. However, once this subject had been settled, it soon moved on to the subject of money, i.e. loaning money to governments to pay for the repatriation of their prisoners-of-war. Sir William Goode explained that the International Committee for Relief Credits would probably consider financing the matter if the countries concerned asked for part of the committee's money to be used for the repatriation of their prisoners-of-war. The International Committee for Relief Credits was a body set up by the governments of the Allied powers and Western neutrals with the intention of rebuilding Europe after the war. It was decided to advise the governments concerned to apply for the first loan of £680,000 in the way proposed by Goode.

Accordingly, Nansen invited the Austrian and Hungarian Governments to apply for £220,000 (30%) each and the Czechoslovak, Yugoslav, Polish and Romanian Governments for £70,000 (10%) each. Nansen also asked the lending governments to agree to these requests.

At the meeting of the Council of the League of Nations on 14 June in London Nansen further urged members to bring pressure to bear on the governments represented on the International Committee for Relief Credits to instruct their delegates to accept Goode's proposal. Moreover, Secretary-General Drummond wrote a letter of encouragement to the heads of each of the lending governments represented on the Committee. The letter to the British Government was addressed to the Prime Minister and its receipt was acknowledged by him.

The British representative at the meeting of the Council, Lord Curzon, in both his private and public speeches encouraged Nansen to believe that the assistance requested would be approved. Convinced that Goode's scheme would work, and trusting in the assurances of goodwill and assistance he received from several prominent members of the British Cabinet, Nansen suspended his search for money elsewhere. He cancelled his appeals to private charities until the question of government loans had been settled.

It was therefore something of a shock when on 2 July a telegram was sent to Nansen from John Gorvin, the Secretary of the International Committee for Relief Credits, stating that the British Treasury's view was that the money should not be diverted from its original purpose, i.e. it would not be available for the repatriation of prisoners-of-war. The British Government was not opposed to funding the repatriation, but did not feel that this committee was the appropriate agency. The French delegate took a similar view. The committee therefore recommended that delegates of lending governments should enter into direct negotiations with the League of Nations and countries requiring the repatriation of prisoners to decide how the money should be raised. This meant that Nansen was no further forward that he had been a month earlier. The loss of every day was of the greatest importance to him, particularly if the prisoners were to be repatriated by the winter of 1920–1921.

Nansen was now in a very difficult position. Either the British Government should instruct its delegate on the Relief Credits Committee to reverse his attitude—and to induce the French delegate to do the same—or they should somehow give instructions to make a comparable sum of money available to Nansen. It had already been shown that the League of Nations was not an aid organization, nor did it have a budget for such initiatives. However, Drummond had spent nineteen years working in the British Foreign Office in Whitehall and had at one time been private secretary to

Arthur Balfour, an influential conservative politician. Drummond now wrote to Balfour: "I should be very grateful if you felt it possible to use your great influence with the Government on Dr Nansen's behalf. It would be rather sad if the League failed in a question which it has assumed a certain responsibility. Would you find it practicable in the circumstances to place Dr Nansen's suggestion before Mr Walter Long?"[31] Balfour had been British Secretary of State during the Treaty of Versailles negotiations and knew Nansen very well. According to Noel-Baker, Balfour wrote "a very strong letter to the Chancellor of the Exchequer" to coincide with the Prime Minister's Cabinet meeting on 15 July. Furthermore, Nansen sent a telegram from Tallinn in Estonia that was read out at this Cabinet meeting with considerable impact. Due to these efforts, on 29 July Nansen received the money he wanted and more—Balfour had asked for the larger amount of £850,000. Noel-Baker thought that the French Government "would follow the lead of the British" and this eventually turned out to be true. The British Government stipulated that "no portion of the fund" should be used for the repatriation of German prisoners.

Although the United Kingdom and Switzerland agreed to release the sums required—on condition that other European States did likewise—it proved difficult to actually lay hands on the cash since the British would not put any money on the table until France and Italy followed suite. Nansen met Balfour on 11 August 1920 and explained the situation. Balfour immediately contacted Austen Chamberlain, the Chancellor of the Exchequer. Thus it was that some money was actually paid into the bank on 20 August. However, the Treasury continued to make difficulties because the other countries did not pay their part fast enough.

Nansen attended another meeting on 12 September in Kaunus, Lithuania, with representatives of Germany, Austria and the international aid agencies. Now that Nansen had been accepted by the Soviet authorities, it was decided that he should lead the repatriation efforts.

When the repatriations began a number of transit camps were set up in the USSR under the authority of Alexander Eiduk. Nansen's team knew that success would depend upon two factors: the efficiency of the Russian railways; and the capacity of shipping in the Eastern Baltic. It turned out that the capacity of the Russian railway system was not as limited as had been anticipated, so that all those prisoners located in European Russia and Western Siberia could be repatriated via the Baltic ports. Trains brought prisoners to a gathering place in Moscow run by the German Soldiers' Council, while one train a day took them on to ports on the Baltic coast where the Red Cross took over. Narva in Estonia quickly became overcrowded and it was apparent that the limiting factor was not the Russian railways, but the number of ships available to pick the men up.

At the beginning of August 1920, Nansen's staff planned for four trains a week from Moscow to Narva in Estonia, two trains a week to Björkö in Finland, and two trains a week to Riga in Latvia, with each train carrying 1,000 passengers. This meant that at least 28,000 men could be repatriated per month. Most of the repatriated Russian soldiers departed from Stettin, at that time the largest German port on the Baltic. A central warehouse for both medication and clothing was located at Stettin.

After the meeting in London in June 1920, the British Admiralty made a number of ships available for a fee, but then began to make difficulties and threatened to withdraw all of the ships—even the four original ones that were already ferrying the men home. Nansen had to intervene forcefully with the British Government to prevent this from happening. By late August there was a complete change of heart by the Admiralty and the British relaxed the "red tape" so that a total of fifteen ships were in operation.[32] The fact that these seized German ships were used for repatriation was a significant element in reducing costs, since Nansen's staff did not have to charter ships on the open market. Another fortunate circumstance was that it would have been very expensive to take out insurance on ships travelling to Russian ports, whereas this did not apply to Estonia and Finland.

For the three-day voyage, the ships were crewed by members of the German Navy and were equipped with beds, kitchens, latrines and stoves for heating. By September 1920 the repatriation operation was functioning to everyone's satisfaction.

In the middle of all this coming and going, Philip Noel-Baker participated in the 1920 Olympic Games being held in Antwerp, Belgium. He was the captain of the British team and carried the national flag during the opening ceremony, winning a silver medal in the 1,500 metres. He is, in fact, the only person to have won an Olympic Medal and also to have been awarded a Nobel Prize.

PROGRESS AT LAST

In October 1920 the League of Nations moved its headquarters to Geneva. In his speech at the first annual Assembly of the League on 18 November 1920[33] Nansen said:

> Never in my life have I been brought into touch with so formidable an amount of suffering as that which I have been called upon to endeavour to alleviate. But this suffering has been only an inevitable result of a war such as that which convulsed the world in 1914. It is right for the League to deal with questions such as that of bringing the prisoners to their homes, but the real lesson which I have learnt from the work which I have undertaken is this—that it is vital for

the League to prevent for evermore a recurrence of catastrophes from which such incalculable human suffering must inevitably result.

The Secretary-General presented a report to the meeting of the Council of the League of Nations on 23 February 1921. He remarked that Nansen did not wish to lay too great a stress on the financial aspects, but the lack of money was a constant source of anxiety. Matters had not developed as desired, and it was now necessary for him to appeal to the Council for their assistance to complete the work with which he had been entrusted. A complete resumé of the position was laid before the Council so that it could consider the steps that should be taken to deal with the financial situation.

The Baltic Routes

By February 1921, 280,000 prisoners of all nationalities had been returned to their respective countries. This figure is impressive inasmuch as, in spite of the great difficulties of transport during the winter months, the weekly average had been well maintained. Owing to ice, however, the ports of Narva and Björkö had been closed and it was necessary either to make use of other ports or to increase the use of railways. A sea route was organized in November from Baltischport (nowadays Paldiski in Estonia) and although at one time it was feared this route would also be closed by ice, this did not happen. Another route from Riga in Latvia was also available. There was a problem, however, in supplying food for the prisoners in transit. Since this had to be purchased on the open market, the small amounts of cash available were hardly sufficient.

Nansen had always wanted to make greater use of railways, but this ambition had been hampered by the unsettled state of affairs in some of the Baltic provinces, particularly in obtaining permission for trains to run through the "Polish corridor."

This problem was addressed at a conference held at Riga on 17 January 1921 at which representatives of the German, Soviet, Polish, Latvian and Lithuanian Governments were present. Nansen was represented by Édouard Frick of the Red Cross. This conference was extraordinarily successful in reaching an agreement between all concerned. As a result, transportation by rail between Russia and the other countries was established. The Lithuanian, Latvian and Polish Governments gave permission for three or four trains per week to cross their territories in each direction.

These arrangements resulted in quicker repatriation and consequent economies. Ships and trains would continue working as long as necessary to carry all the men home. It was hoped that no man would be delayed by transport difficulties upon reaching his own country.

A further report was submitted by Nansen to the Council of the League of Nations.[34] In it, he said that the total number of prisoners of all nationalities repatriated by the Baltic route up to 1 June 1921 amounted to approximately 323,850 men.

The Black Sea Routes

Owing to the very disturbed political situation in the Black Sea and Caucasian provinces, there was considerable difficulty in obtaining reliable information concerning the numbers and whereabouts of prisoners in the region. In consequence, Nansen sent a special Red Cross mission there in December 1920 in order to look into the position. Previous to the departure of this mission, an agreement was made with the Soviet Government whereby prisoners in Turkmenistan should be collected and transported by rail to Moscow, from whence they would be channelled through the Baltic routes. This plan worked satisfactorily and about 5,000 prisoners passed through immediately. It was estimated that a further 12,000 men still remained in Turkmenistan.

The Red Cross mission reported on its activities in the Caucasian region. Following the complete breakdown of all rail transport and the political disorganization of these territories, it was impossible to deal with prisoners from these regions in the same way as those from Turkmenistan. As far as the Red Cross Mission could ascertain, there were about 15,000 prisoners waiting to take this route, of whom 2,000 were at Novorossiysk on the Black Sea. The first steamer brought 14,089 prisoners of many different nationalities from Novorossiysk to Trieste. It was reported that some prisoners, principally Austrians and Hungarians, were being forced to join various revolutionary armies within Russia, thus making it even more difficult to obtain information about the numbers to be repatriated.

Vladivostok

According to the information available when Nansen made his preliminary estimates of the total cost of repatriation, there were about 15,000 prisoners who needed transportation from Eastern Siberia. Some US$3 million promised by the American Red Cross would allow ships to repatriate these Austrians and Hungarians. This route was obviously the most complicated and expensive of all, since the voyage from Vladivostok to Trieste took forty days. The final number of prisoners conveyed from Vladivostok was 11,080 who were all returned to their native countries.[35]

NANSENHILFE

While the Russian prisoners-of-war held in Germany were receiving American aid under the leadership of Herbert Hoover, for the men held in Russia and Siberia the situation was not the same. Even though the Red Cross had a number of representatives in the USSR, they could not possibly feed and clothe all of the remaining prisoners-of-war during the winter of 1920–1921. There was clearly the need for an organization to provide supplies to them.

Since the Russians did not recognize the League of Nations, any organization providing relief had to be politically neutral. Beyond his duties in repatriating prisoners-of-war, Nansen became involved in an independent charity organization called Nansenhilfe [Nansen Aid] which provided money, food, medicine and clothing to those held captive in Russia. This body was formally founded at the meeting of September 1920 in Kaunas, Lithuania, between Nansen, the German and Soviet authorities, and a number of non-governmental aid organizations. As usual, the Soviets took advantage of the meeting to air a number of grievances about the way they were being treated by Western governments.

Previously, on 24 August Nansen had sent a number of telegrams to non-governmental aid organizations suggesting that their scattered efforts to help prisoners in Russia would have more impact if he co-ordinated them. Thus, all the different NGOs were asked to communicate with a headquarters established in Berlin.

Moritz Schlesinger, who was in charge of the German department responsible for prisoners-of-war, realised that it would be impossible for all of the prisoners to reach home from Siberia before the winter of 1920–1921 and therefore it was necessary to provide food, clothing and medicine to them. Nansen was of the opinion that it was more efficient to concentrate all resources on bringing the men home rather than on providing supplies. However, it was evident that not all of them could be repatriated in the short term and aid measures would raise the moral of the prisoners. The result was that Nansen would not divert money from the repatriation fund, but was prepared to accept Schlesinger's proposal and to participate in it. Nansen contacted the Soviet authorities who accepted to distribute aid to foreign prisoners held in Russia on condition that this was under the control of Alexander Eiduk's Centroevak organization and local Russian staff. This condition was accepted both by Nansen and Schlesinger—and also by Western public opinion.

Although the headquarters of Nansenhilfe was located in Berlin, daily operations were co-ordinated by a working group in Geneva. In Moscow there was a central distribution committee, with local committees situated in different parts of Russia. Nansenhilfe distributed money, food, clothing and medical supplies, as well as gift packages from NGOs coming from all parts of the world. Despite the fact that they would not grant entry permits for foreigners, the Soviet authorities turned out to be surprisingly co-operative and competent.

Nansen had lent his name to an organization created on German initiative—a unique event in contemporary humanitarian organizations. The choice of name reflects the aura of Nansen's personality and the fact that he was politically neutral—he was not associated with any Western government, was even considered independent of the League of Nations and negotiated with the Soviet authorities as an individual. In this political vacuum it was believed that Nansen's name would expedite the distribution of aid. It was also probable that the use of his name encouraged contributions from sources that otherwise might have refused to deal directly with a German initiative. Nansen was able to observe himself how aid should be distributed, which would come in useful in the very near future.

Money, clothing, food, gifts and other supplies came from a variety of sources to the 40,000 prisoners-of-war remaining in Russia. We may mention particularly the American and Canadian YMCAs, and the Hungarian Government.[36]

SUCCESS

In addition to the work directly connected with his own plans, Nansen had been obliged to intervene in other repatriation efforts. He obtained the release and repatriation of some Americans from Russia, and also a certain number of French prisoners from Baku in Azerbaijan. The settlement of a longstanding dispute between the Greek and Bulgarian Governments over the exchange of prisoners was settled by Nansen through the dispatch of a Red Cross mission to these countries. Through Nansen's intervention an agreement was reached between the Hungarian and Romanian Governments for a final exchange of prisoners. It was anticipated that all outstanding questions relating to prisoners-of-war in these countries would be completed by the middle of 1922.

A key player in the repatriation of prisoners-of-war was Édouard Frick. In 1918 he had been the Red Cross delegate at Petrograd in Russia and as of January 1919 he was appointed head of the new Assistance Mission for Russia.

While Nansen's High Commission provided financial and political support, most of the practical work was carried out by the Red Cross. When the newly released prisoners reached Berlin, Björkö, Narva, Riga, Stettin or Swinemunde, they were housed in temporary accommodation managed by the Red Cross. In charge of each camp was a Swiss citizen who was a delegate of the Red Cross. Even the doctors were Swiss citizens. The Red Cross staff in each camp were responsible for supervising the prisoners, verifying their nationality, ensuring the security of the camps, and generally facilitating transportation. Upon arrival at the camps the prisoners were given a medical examination, disinfected, fed and given a clean set of clothes. Governments were wary of transmitting epidemics, both physical and ideological.

The purpose of determining the prisoners' nationality was so that the cost of repatriation could be distributed proportionally. A significant point here is that the Red Cross issued temporary identity documents for many of the prisoners—a clear forerunner of the subsequent Nansen Passport.

WHO GETS THE CREDIT?

The whole operation took more than two years to accomplish. In his final report to the third annual Assembly in 1922, Nansen was able to state that 427,866 prisoners of nearly thirty different nationalities had been repatriated; of these, over 250,000 were Russians.[37] The Fifth Committee paid a fitting tribute to Nansen's achievement:

> The Council of the League of Nations, by a resolution dated 11th April 1920 entrusted Dr Nansen with the duty of coordinating all the efforts which hitherto had been made to help prisoners-of-war and to achieve their repatriation. Dr Nansen, to whose active love of humanity no appeal is ever made in vain, accepted this heavy responsibility. At that time, many experienced men considered him rash; the work was so immense and the resources almost nonexistent. The most optimistic considered that part only of the soldiers could be repatriated and that even this would take many years and only be achieved at enormous cost. On 1st July 1922 Dr Nansen had completed this repatriation and the funds at his disposal had not exceeded 400,000 British pounds.

When there were no ships, Nansen found ships. When the mistrust of the Soviet Government was at its height, Nansen secured its goodwill. The International Committee for Relief Credit could only furnish limited sums of money, but Nansen spent less than £1 for each life saved; all the money came in the form of loans. Nansen secured so much help, so much goodwill and so much co-operation that the mere lack of money could not stop him. One month after his appointment as High Commissioner the transport of prisoners began. By September 1920 100,000 prisoners-of-war had been repatriated and this number rose to 280,000 by February 1921. By March 1922 there remained some 4,000 stragglers, some of whom were either difficult to reach or not anxious to return. On this account the activities of the repatriation organization were maintained until 1 July 1922. The few hundred men who did not avail themselves of this opportunity could still be repatriated through the regular transport system.

Nansen himself stressed that it was a first-rate example of fruitful co-operation. He expressed his gratitude to the Red Cross for its support in all matters concerning the repatriation of prisoners-of-war. Without the network of relief workers and the infrastructure provided by the Red Cross and the other voluntary organizations, the task would have been impossible. It could even be said that the Red Cross did the work and the League of Nations took the credit. People like Philip Noel-Baker wanted to show that the League had the liberty of action that individual countries did not have, that it could serve a purpose and therefore was needed. It is evident that without Nansen's passion and his ability to overcome obstacles, the operation would not have been as successful as it was. It is also true to say that both the Soviet and German authorities were very keen to see this operation carried out success-fully and contributed to its completion. However, such was the political climate at the time that neither the Soviet nor the German Governments benefited directly from the loan arrangements.

The High Commissioner of the League of Nations, assisted by the Red Cross and other charitable organizations relieved the Allied Powers of a politically awkward task. The success of the operation to repatriate the pris-oners-of-war after the First World War was the League's first great humani-tarian task and greatly enhanced the prestige of the new organization, making it widely known and admired.

NOTES

1. Memo 184489/W/57, box R–1474, League of Nations Archives. [All League of Nations documents are copyright: United Nations Archives, Geneva.]
2. Report written by Crowdy, ref. 40/3179, box R–1574, League of Nations Archives.
3. Doc. 2792, box R–1574, League of Nations Archives.
4. Report written by Crowdy, ref. 40/3179, box R–1574, League of Nations Archives.
5. Ibid.
6. Minutes of second session of the Council of the League of Nations, League of Nations Archives.
7. Memorandum 3052, box R–1574, League of Nations Archives.
8. Memorandum from Drummond to his colleagues concerning prisoners-of-war, doc. 40/3161/792, box R–1574, League of Nations Archives.
9. Letter to Henderson, ref. 40/3053/2792, box R–1574, League of Nations Archives.
10. Doc. 3179, box R–1574, League of Nations Archives.
11. Doc. 40/3713/2729 box, R–1475, League of Nations Archives.
12. Doc. 40/3653/2792, box R–1475, League of Nations Archives.
13. Ibid.
14. Doc. 40/3808/2792, box R–1475, League of Nations Archives.
15. Doc 40/3850/2792, box R–1475, League of Nations Archives.
16. Ibid.
17. Doc. 40/3890/2792, box R–1475, League of Nations Archives.
18. Ibid.
19. Ibid.

20. Huntford, R. *Nansen: The Explorer as hero,* p. 601. London: Abacus, 1997.

21. Whittaker, D.J. *Fighter for Peace: Philip Noel-Baker, 1889–1982,* p. 48. York, UK: William Sessions Ltd., 1989.

22. Huntford, p. 602.

23. Nansen's first report is dated 28 May, doc. 40/4606/2792, box R–1476, League of Nations Archives.

24. Ibid.

25. Doc. 40/4078/2792, box R–1474, League of Nations Archives.

26. Doc. 40/4459/2792, box R–1475, League of Nations Archives.

27. Ibid.

28. Huntford, p. 606.

29. Doc. 40/4372/2792, box R–1475, League of Nations Archives.

30. Doc. 40/4606/2792 and 40/4836/2792, box R–1475, League of Nations Archives.

31. Letter from Drummond to Balfour dated 2 June 1920, ref. 40/4525/2792, box R–1475, League of Nations Archives.

32. Huntford, p. 607.

33. Records of the first Assembly of the League of Nations, 1920, League of Nations Archives.

34. Missions of the third Session of the Council, League of Nations Archives.

35. Records of the second Assembly of the League of Nations, 1921, pp. 105–106, League of Nations Archives.

36. Concerning Nansenhilfe and its work, we received much valuable information from Carl Emil Vogt.

37. Records of the third Assembly of the League of Nations, 1922, pp. 105–106, League of Nations Archives.

Chapter Four

The Russian Revolution
and Its Aftermath

DISCONTENT IN RUSSIA

In 1915 during the First World War, the German Army turned its full attention to the Eastern Front. The Germans were better led, better trained and better supplied than the Russian Army. By the end of October 1916 Russia had lost nearly 5 million men as casualties or as prisoners-of-war. Heavy casualties gave strength to the impression that Tsar Nicholas II was unfit to rule the country. The neglected soldiers began to turn against the imperial family.

As the war progressed, royalist officers were killed and were replaced with soldiers rising up through the ranks with little loyalty to the Tsar. These men, usually of peasant or worker backgrounds, were to play a major role in the politicization of the troops in 1917.

There were no less than two Russian Revolutions in 1917. Nicholas II abdicated and was replaced by a provisional government in the first revolution of February 1917 focused around Petrograd. In the ensuing chaos, members of the Imperial Parliament or Duma formed the Russian Provisional Government. The more radical socialist factions or soviets could count upon the allegiance of the lower classes and the political left. A period of dual power ensued, during which the Provisional Government tried to govern the country tolerated by the national network of soviets. In the second revolution during October, the Bolshevik party, led by Vladimir Lenin and the workers' soviets, overthrew the Provisional Government in Petrograd.

To bring a rapid end to Russia's participation in the First World War, the Bolshevik leaders signed the Treaty of Brest-Litovsk with Germany, Austro-Hungary and their allies, and also with Ottoman Turkey in March 1918. A

Civil War then erupted between the "Red" (Bolshevik) and "White" (anti-Bolshevik) factions, which was to continue until the summer of 1920 with the Bolsheviks ultimately victorious.

When the Big Four—Clemenceau, Lloyd George, Orlando and Wilson—met in January 1919 at the Paris Peace Conference, new nations were ready to emerge. Russia had lost large parts of its territory: the Baltic States, Ukraine, Armenia, Georgia, Azerbaijan and Dagestan were all now ready to declare their independence. Lloyd George, as we have already stated in Chapter II, would have preferred representatives of the Russian Government to be present, but this proved to be impossible.[1] European politicians were very wary of Bolshevism, while the Bolsheviks themselves showed no enthusiasm to participate.[2] With the Civil War taking place in Russia, who actually represented the country?[3]

The Allied Powers had set up an ambitious programme for the Peace Conference, and were hoping to re-organize the world. However, the problems they encountered were far more complex that they could ever have anticipated. The First World War had already given rise to the Russian Revolution, severe unemployment and a flood of refugees. Facing domestic pressure, events they could not control and conflicting claims they could not reconcile, the negotiators were in the end simply overwhelmed—and made quick deals and compromises reaching unsatisfying conclusions that would echo down throughout the history of the twentieth century.[4]

The dramatic political upheavals taking place in Russia during 1917–1920 produced enormous numbers of refugees either by displacing them internally or by forcing them to leave the country in order to escape the Revolution and the Civil War. Many Russian refugees believed their exile to be a temporary situation; they expected that the imminent overthrow or collapse of the Bolshevik state would allow them to return home. They were mistaken. Refugees faced definitive exile amid military dangers and economic insecurity. However, before the League of Nations could turn its attention to the plight of these refugees, another far more serious problem arose.

FAMINE IN RUSSIA

On 13 July 1921 Nansen, along with other prominent people such as Herbert Hoover, received a telegram purportedly from Maxim Gorky, the celebrated Russian writer. It contained the first news of calamitous crop failures in central Russia, the North Caucasus and the Ukraine following the worst drought in 150 years. In fact, the drought had destroyed the crops for two years in a row—1920 and 1921. The Communist regime had chosen this method of communication since it had no diplomatic relations with the outside world. In the following days other telegrams followed signed by Lenin and Foreign Minister Chicherin, this time addressed to the world's governments.

The drought was compounded by the impact of the First World War, the Revolution, the Civil War, the seizure of grain (particularly seed grain) by the Bolshevik and the White Russian armies, and the Allied military intervention. With the destruction of infrastructures and communications in Russia, social organization had collapsed, particularly in the countryside. In the Volga basin and in the Ukraine people were starving to death. Epidemics had broken out and the area was in a state of disaster. Estimates indicated that 30 million people were affected. Whereas, in normal circumstances, a famine in one part of the country might be alleviated by a surplus elsewhere, the collapse of the transport system meant that grain could not be moved. After the famine was over a Russian official admitted that the problem was caused "more by an unequal distribution of cereals than by a true shortage."

Famine in Russia was by no means an unknown phenomenon. Since the mid-nineteenth century there had been several failed harvests followed by famine, the worst of which took place in 1891–1892. Russian agriculture was vulnerable to unstable weather patterns because of old-fashioned farming methods and the division of land into tiny subsistence farms. On the other hand, population growth was high. Attempts at reform had had little effect and in many places the Tsar's regime had insisted on maintaining the feudal system intact.

To Nansen the problem of the famine in Russia was even more important than that of the refugees. It will be recalled that Hoover had used Nansen as an intermediary to approach the Soviet Government in the early part of 1919 about supplying food with a view to influencing the political situation in Russia, but the Soviets had rejected it. [5] Now Nansen replied to Gorky that the only people who could supply food to the famine-stricken areas were the Americans, but since American citizens were detained in Russia, such assistance was unlikely. On his own initiative, Nansen sent a large supply of salted fish with the proviso that a Norwegian citizen nominated by him should supervise its distribution. There was also a reaction from John Gorvin of the International Committee of Relief Credits who had worked with Nansen on the repatriation of prisoners of war. Gorvin wrote to Nansen suggesting that he should be the international figure who would persuade the European and American governments to send food to the Russians. Gorvin's request led to an immediate reaction from Nansen: "Your letter has thrown a new match into my soul."

Meanwhile, Herbert Hoover offered to help the Russians through the American Relief Administration (ARA) and—unexpectedly—the Russians accepted! After ten days of stressful negotiations, an agreement was signed by Maxim Litvinov for the Russians and Walter Lyman Brown for the ARA on 20 August 1921 in Riga, the Latvian capital. This accord gave the ARA complete independence to manage its own affairs in the distribution of food using its own staff, on condition that it would not meddle in Russian politics. Seven Americans held in Russia were released. It is noteworthy that Hoover did not envisage co-operating with the Europeans or the League of Nations on the supply of food. There was at this time a grain surplus in the United States.

On the same day as the signing of the ARA agreement, thanks to more behind-the-scenes manoeuvring by Philip Noel-Baker, Nansen was invited to another meeting in Riga called by the International Committee of the Red Cross (ICRC). The President of the ICRC, the former President of Switzerland, Gustave Ador, had taken the initiative to convene a conference of voluntary organizations which was also attended by representatives of a number of governments. This conference asked Nansen to take charge of the relief efforts under the aegis of an organization called the International Committee for Aid to Russia (CISR—Le Comité international de secours à la Russie), a federation of charities. Nansen willingly assumed the post of High Commissioner for Relief on behalf of the ICRC and the voluntary relief organizations (and not, therefore, on behalf of the League of Nations). Herbert Hoover had also been asked to assume the task jointly with Nansen or to nominate another commissioner, but Hoover declined because he was already running the ARA relief operation—he also had little faith in the CISR. Therefore, Nansen became the sole High Commissioner for the CISR. Thus it was that one man would be responsible for both the prisoners-of-war programme and combating the Russian famine and, as we shall see, the Russian refugees.

Nansen's colleagues, the treasurer Thomas Lodge, John Gorvin, Édouard Frick and Moritz Schlesinger, had already planned a visit to Russia to inspect the prisoner-of-war camps. They were to be accompanied by William Andrew Mackenzie of the Save the Children Fund. Nansen had originally declined to accompany them, but now that he had become involved in famine relief he changed his mind. During his meeting with Litvinov in Riga, Nansen suggested that he should be invited to Russia to see for himself the situation on the ground. Litvinov was lukewarm about the visit saying that there was no famine in Moscow, but he obtained travel permits enabling them to meet once again the Soviet Commissioner for Foreign Affairs, Georgy Chicherin. When in Moscow, Nansen discussed the provision of supplies and the raising of credits for the transportation and distribution of food through an agreement under the supervision of a newly-created International Russian Relief Committee. The matter of Russian refugees was also raised. Nansen signed an agreement on the implementation of relief efforts with Chicherin. All authority would be in the joint hands of a representative of the Soviet Government and a representative appointed by Nansen. Distribution of relief would be undertaken by the existing Soviet infrastructure.

This arrangement can be contrasted with the one negotiated by Litvinov and Brown which placed all responsibility in the hands of the Americans. At this time, public opinion in Europe had a very low opinion of co-operation with the Bolsheviks and Nansen's agreement was very poorly received. Nevertheless, Nansen left Moscow full of enthusiasm to search for money.

Meanwhile, "with a great deal of difficulty," Philip Noel-Baker had persuaded Secretary-General Drummond that the repatriation of prisoners-of-war, the famine in Russia and the Russian refugee crisis should be dealt with together. Drummond was not convinced that the League's intervention would be useful. Nevertheless, a meeting at the League of Nations in Geneva on 22–23 August 1921 accepted Noel-Baker's idea.

THE SEARCH FOR FUNDS

Many European governments remained sceptical about Nansen's relief efforts and were reluctant to provide loans. In London, some British politicians (such as the Prime Minister Lloyd George) and some newspapers supported Nansen's request for money. Others had little sympathy, believing that he had simply been comprehensively duped by the Russians. If he wanted money, they said, Nansen would have to find it from private sources. While millions of people were dying of hunger, the British and French Governments prevaricated, saying that proper accounting methods would have to be respected. Philip Noel-Baker observed with scorn the lamentable quibbling over money equivalent to "half a battleship."[6]

The Allied Supreme Council had established an International Commission for Russian Relief which met in Paris on 30 August 1921. To begin with, the delegates criticized Nansen for having reached such a facile agreement with the Soviet authorities. The Commission decided that no aid would be provided until a thirty-member team had been admitted to Russia to inspect the situation on the ground. Predictably, the Russians immediately rejected this proposal. After two more meetings, this commission dissolved itself without taking action of any kind.

A new strategy was devised in an attempt to force governments to lend the money that would overcome the famine. Nansen would travel to Russia and visit the famine-stricken areas, returning with an eye-witness account and photographs that would shock public opinion and governments into action. He returned from this journey on Christmas Day, 1921, and then set out on a lecture tour covering cities in the United Kingdom, France, the Netherlands, Switzerland and Scandinavia. While his presentation had a significant impact and sizeable sums of money were collected from the audiences, governments remained indifferent. Despite behind-the-scenes activity by Lord Robert Cecil and Philip Noel-Baker, the British Parliament decided not to provide any credits in a vote which took place on 9 March 1922. Other Western governments—even Norway—were reluctant to become involved in any dealings with the Soviets and followed the same policy. In due course, the Norwegian Government relented and granted 3 million Norwegian kroner to relief efforts—no doubt in sympathy with Nansen's unique position. The Norwegian Red Cross also played an active role in relief initiatives throughout the period, providing personnel, food and generous gifts of money.

Nansen then appealed to private organizations for the help that had been withheld by governments. He sent the following telegram to the Save the Children International Union:

> Hundreds of thousands of Russian children are dying of hunger, and millions of others are threatened with the same fate. Convinced that only an unprecedented effort, immediately undertaken can save them, I request the Save the Children International Union to appeal to men, women, and especially to children to give quickly all that they can economize, to save the little famished ones in Russia. Never, in the history of the world has help been more desperately needed. Every minute is precious.

The response to Nansen's request for funds from private donors was good. Fifteen countries made a united effort to help the Russians through the Save the Children Fund, but it was a poor substitute for what could have been done if national governments had taken his appeal to heart. With the help of the former Red Cross delegate Édouard Frick, with whom Nansen had worked closely during the repatriation of the prisoner-of-war, he built up an organization to provide aid, with John Gorvin as his agent in Moscow. It was responsible for the purchase of flour, meat, blankets and medicine, and for delivery vans to undertake transport, organizing co-operative efforts with the central authorities in Russia and co-ordinating the work of the many private relief organizations. Nansen's other praiseworthy colleague was a Russian-speaking Norwegian Army officer, Vidkun Quisling, who ran the aid organization in the Ukraine with military efficiency. (This is the same Quisling whose name would in the Second World War become a synonym for traitor!) In 1924 Noel-Baker accepted a chair at the London School of Economics. The result was that Quisling would eventually become Nansen's secretary, but did not occupy a position comparable to that of the invaluable Noel-Baker.

Nansen's wife Sigrun complained that he had become "an idiotic Good Samaritan," while Western governments became suspicious that his activities were being used by the Russians to exploit the famine for political purposes. Without being aware of it, Nansen had become an unpaid public relations officer for the Soviets. For instance, Nansen appeared to be buying grain on the London market, whereas his name was being used without his knowledge on transactions designed to overcome the trade embargo with Russia. When he declared that the salvation of the West would come out of Russia, the ICRC panicked and tried to play down its association with him.

A British inspector, Sir Benjamin Robertson, who examined the work of various charities in Russia, came to the conclusion that Nansen's efforts to distribute food to the starving were not as efficient as they might be. John Gorvin did not speak Russian and the Moscow office had no idea where its supplies of food had gone. Even Frick was disappointed with the performance of the Moscow office.

THE LEAGUE FAILS TO ACT

During 1921 and 1922, several attempts were made by the British politicians Lord Robert Cecil and Arthur Balfour, as well as Drummond's assistant Philip Noel-Baker, to oblige the League of Nations to intervene in the Russian famine. Two Norwegian Foreign Ministers, Arnold Ræstad and Johan Mowinckel, also suggested that the League should set up a commission and publish a report on the situation. But since the Russians themselves refused to enter into any form of co-operation with the League, all these efforts were in vain.

When the second Assembly of the League of Nations opened on 5 September 1921 Nansen was to spend nearly a month in Geneva. He made a long speech (written by Noel-Baker) explaining the Russian situation.[7] The Swiss delegate, Guiseppe Motta, expressed the feelings that the League of Nations could not intervene in the internal affairs of any government, so any aid must come from charitable organizations. Aristide Briand, the French Prime Minister, pinpointed the dilemma: how could anyone save the victims of famine without the Soviet Government profiting from the situation to consolidate its position? The feeling among Western governments was that any aid could be interpreted as political support for tragic mismanagement by an incompetent regime.

To the question, will the USSR keep its promises?—Nansen replied:

> I have worked with the Soviet Government now for more than a year in connection with the repatriation of prisoners, and I must say that, in spite of numerous difficulties, the Soviet Government has actually kept all its obligations and all its agreements and promises it has made to me and to my organization. As far as transport is concerned it has agreed, for instance, during a certain period, that 4,000 prisoners a week should be sent out. I said: "It's impossible for you to do it now that you are carrying on a war with Poland." They said: "We will do it." And they actually did do it. In fact, to my annoyance, they did more than their promise so that one camp at one time had considerably more prisoners than the available accommodation.

He gave the example of a special organization formed for helping prisoners in Russia, which had sent clothing for 60,000 prisoners—coats, shoes, underwear, etc.—articles which were of the highest value, and which could have been sold for a fortune in Russia. "Yet," he declared, "not a single article was lost inside the borders of Russia." Nansen concluded his speech as follows:

> We know that at least 20 million people are starving; we know that everything necessary to save them is within a few hundred miles. We know that only one thing is required, for one part of the human race to organize and help the other suffering part. The cost of armaments to the members of the League is hundreds of millions of pounds a year, and that's to defend them against political dangers. Less than ten percent of this in the form of a loan only to Russia will prevent appalling disaster and avert the greatest of all political dangers.

Nansen's suggestion that the League should relieve the Russian famine by grants in kind and by guaranteeing a loan was referred to the Sixth Committee[8] which decided that, as several governments declined to approve official credits, the responsibility of the League in the matter was at an end. It should be pointed out that the League of Nations was not a charitable organization and once again political considerations had blocked the way. This partial defeat was a bitter disappointment to Nansen. He was a stranger to failure and the adamant refusal of the League of Nations to help was a setback. He felt that the League had missed a golden opportunity. "I cannot think that right; I cannot think it wise; I cannot think it anything but a disastrous mistake."[9]

Furthermore, Nansen became the victim of a vicious campaign of slander. Russian émigré circles in France, the United Kingdom, Finland and other countries accused Nansen of being a Bolshevik and acting as Lenin's undercover agent. They demanded that he be dismissed from the post of High Commissioner. This placed Nansen in a great dilemma because he had to maintain good relations with the Soviet authorities for famine relief, while by this time he had also been made responsible for protecting Russian refugees.[10]

On 30 September 1921 he spoke out about the difficulties that were being put in the way of even such private relief as had been given: "We are doing what we can through private charity, but even our charity . . . is very seriously impeded by the campaign of misrepresentation which is being carried on."

> There are any amount of lies being circulated. I may remind you of one story that went to the papers, which you will remember, namely that the first train that Mr Hoover sent in to feed the Russians was looted by the Soviet Army in Russia. It was a lie, but still the same story was repeated over and over again in the press of Europe. I was abused for having sent an expedition to Siberia, and I know it was said that I was bringing arms for a revolution. It was a lie, but I have read it in the papers. It is said that my friend Captain Sverdrup was in

command of it, but all that he was doing was carrying agricultural machinery to Siberia. That was not so very dangerous after all. There are many similar stories being circulated. [...] I think I know what the underlying thought in this campaign is. It is this: that the action which we propose will, if it succeeds, strengthen the Soviet Government. I think that that is a mistake. I do not think that we shall strengthen the Soviet Government by showing the Russian people that there are hearts in Europe, and that there are people there ready to help the starving Russian people. But supposing that it does strengthen the Soviet Government? Is there any member of this Assembly who is prepared to say that rather than help the Soviet Government he will allow 20 million people to starve to death? I challenge this Assembly to answer that question.

Nansen described his position with passion: "The mandate I received from the Conference for which I asked is to go on appealing to the governments of the world. I shall go on and try to rouse the countries of Europe to avert the greatest horror in history."

I believe, whatever this Assembly may decide, we shall be able to do something to alleviate the dire distress which exists. But it is a terrible race we are running with the Russian winter, which is already silently and persistently approaching from the north. Soon the waters of Russia will be frozen; soon transport will be hampered by frozen snow. Shall we allow the winter to silence forever 3 million voices which are crying out to us for help? There is still time, but there is not much time left. Do try to imagine what it will be when the Russian winter will set in earnest and try to realise what it means when no food is left, and the whole population is wandering through the barren land in search of food—men, women, children dropping dead by thousands in the frozen snow of Russia. Try to realise what this means, and if you have ever known what it is to fight against hunger, and to fight against the ghastly forces of winter, you will realise what it means and understand what the situation will be. I am convinced you cannot sit still and answer with a cold heart that you are sorry and cannot help. In the name of humanity, in the name of everything noble and sacred to us, I appeal to you who have women and children of your own, to consider what it means to see women and children perishing by starvation. In this place I appeal to the governments, to the governments of Europe, to the whole world for help. Hasten to act before it is too late to repent.

In letters and speeches Lord Robert Cecil staunchly defended Nansen saying that it was ridiculous to imagine him as a tool of the Soviet Government:

People have not hesitated to suggest, so I am told, that Dr Nansen is moved by nationalist feelings on behalf of Norway, and even by personal motives. It is well to state publicly that, in all this matter, Dr Nansen is acting absolutely without any salary of any kind. Other people have alleged that he is engaged in some obscure political intrigue. To us who know Dr Nansen, all this is not more contemptible than it is absurd. We know that it is utterly untrue. We know that it is not only but fantastically untrue.

Nansen's speech was rewarded with great applause—but little else. At that time there were few and poorly coordinated mechanisms for famine relief. He was extremely annoyed about the League of Nations' bureaucratic and heartless attitude to human suffering. He was of the opinion that resources should be a political matter, a part of the politics for a better and more equitable world. Reproached for being naïve and with no understanding of *Realpolitik*, Nansen dashingly replied with his well-known motto: "Charity is *Realpolitik*." Many years later, Philip Noel-Baker had this to say in defence of Nansen's attitude:

> We have listened to the realists for twenty years; on every serious issue they have been wrong. [...] They were wrong for the narrowest and meanest of reasons; because they thought evil more real than good; because they believed in the folly and cowardice and greed of human beings more than in their courage, their generosity, their love of justice and their common sense. [11]

In 1926, Nansen became Rector of St Andrews University in Scotland. In his installation speech expressing his own ideas (but actually written by Philip Noel-Baker and Leonard Woolf—the husband of Virginia Woolf), he once more uttered his disgust at so-called international solidarity:

> Let me, however, give you another example: the Russian famine in 1921–22 when the Volga region and the most fertile parts of Russia were ravaged by a terrible drought—when something like 30 million people or more were starving and dying—dying by the thousand. [...] A heart-rending appeal for help went out to all the world and eventually a great many people in this and in other countries helped, and helped generously. But many more were busy trying to find out first who was to blame. Was it the drought? Or was it the political system of the Russian State? As if that could ameliorate the terrible suffering or make any difference whatever to those who were dying of starvation. But what was worse, there was in various transatlantic countries such an abundance of maize at that time that the farmers did not know how to get rid of it before the new harvest, so they had to burn it as fuel in their railway engines. At the same time the ships in Europe were all idle, and laid up for there were no cargoes. Simultaneously there were thousands, nay millions of unemployed. All this while thirty million people in the Volga region, not far away and easily reached by means of our ships, were allowed to starve and die. The politicians of the world at large, except in the United States, were trying to find an excuse for doing nothing on the pretext that it was the Russians' own fault—a result of the Bolshevik system.

Nansen pointed out that if the unemployed had been put on board the idle ships, the ships had been sent to South America and had brought the excess maize to the Black Sea, and saved the stricken millions, how much suffering could they have relieved. He said: "I tell you that there is something rotten in the condition of the world. There is still ample room for improvements."

LESSONS LEARNED

By September 1922, the Soviet authorities declared that the crisis was over and sought to hasten the departure of foreign aid organizations. The Soviets announced that they were in a position to start exporting grain again. In fact, in November 1921, while travelling by ship from Constantinople to Italy, Nansen was dismayed to learn that the Russians were already exporting grain.

The CISR was disbanded and the High Commission for famine relief closed. However, Nansen and his co-workers continued providing food under the name of "Nansen Aid" until the next harvest was gathered. He invited other organizations, such as the Save the Children Fund and the Quakers, to join him, but they preferred to negotiate separate agreements with the Soviet authorities.

The ARA closed its aid programme in the summer of 1923.[12] Nansen decided to do exactly the same thing, but John Gorvin and a small secretariat stayed in Moscow until the end of 1924. Their work became less concerned with famine relief and more with Russian refugees. It was expected that the Soviet authorities would move rapidly to close down these offices, but they did not do so.

Hoover and the ARA had accomplished a great deal more than Nansen. The ARA worked with great efficiency and had the financial clout to bring Russian bureaucracy to heel. At one stage the ARA was feeding 11 million people on a daily basis in the Volga district, in the Ukraine, the Crimea and Georgia, whereas Nansen's people were catering to about 500,000. It is estimated that the ARA, with an initial budget of $20 million, supplied 80% of the aid provided to the Russians affected by the drought and famine. Russian propaganda afterwards portrayed Nansen as uniquely responsible for foreign aid, although his contribution has been put at only 13%.[13] Since Hoover's accomplishments tended to show the Soviet regime in a bad light, no effort was spared by Russian propaganda to promote Nansen's activities and to obscure those of Hoover.[14] In spite of the wide-scale help that was given, several million people died of hunger and disease in the famine-stricken areas.

Nansen understood that the famine in Russia had contributed to making an unstable situation worse. The priority was to stabilize the USSR and to create the infrastructures that would ensure the problem would not arise again. For this purpose, already in 1922, at the suggestion of Noel-Baker, Nansen had urged the British Government to recognize the Soviet regime. It was not until 1 February 1924 that the United Kingdom actually acknowl-edged the new government of the USSR, being followed shortly thereafter by most of the other European powers; by Japan in January 1925; and by the United States in November 1933.

ONCE MORE, NANSEN INTERVENES

Well before the repatriation of prisoners-of-war was completed and the Russian famine was over, Nansen had been asked to undertake the more difficult task of finding a solution to the Russian refugees fleeing the Soviet regime and the fighting connected with the Civil War. Some significant work had already been undertaken to relieve their distress by voluntary organizations, such as various Red Cross societies, the American Relief Administration and the Save the Children Fund.

A telegram from Gustave Ador, in his capacity as the President of the International Committee of the Red Cross, brought this matter to the attention of the thirteenth session of the Council of the League of Nations on 20 February 1921.[15]

> I beg you on behalf of the International Red Cross to convey to the Council the gratitude of the International Committee of the Red Cross for the great work which you have done to enable us to bring the repatriation of prisoners to a satisfactory conclusion. Thanks to the energy and devotion of your commissioner, Dr Nansen, the problem is now almost solved and all the prisoners are on their way homeward.
>
> This magnificent success encourages us to submit to you a fresh proposal which you will find more fully treated in a memorandum drawn up by the International Red Cross after consultation with the most important organizations which are already taking part on relief work among Russian refugees.

In the memorandum to which Ador refers in his telegram, there is a report of an unofficial meeting that took place on 16 and 17 February 1921 on the subject of Russian refugees. It confirms that at least 800,000 of them were dispersed throughout the countries of Eastern Europe, in particular in the Baltic States, Poland, Bulgaria and Yugoslavia, as well as in Turkey. The legal status of these people was vague and the majority of them were without means of subsistence. Particular attention was drawn to the children and young people among them who were growing up in ever-increasing wretchedness and without education.

The Council of the League of Nations addressed the problem, destined to become tiresomely familiar, of what to do about the Russian refugees.[16] The Council proposed to appoint a commissioner to define the legal position of the Russian refugees wherever they were located without any reference to political concerns. It was considered unacceptable that in the twentieth century there should be such a huge number of men, women and children living in Europe unprotected by any system recognized by international law.

In his telegram Ador stressed the three main aspects of the situation: the legal status of the refugees; their repatriation, their emigration or the organization of their employment in the countries where they are now residing;

and finally the urgent question of material relief due to the deplorable condition in which most of the refugees were living.

The Council chairman, Gabriel Hanotaux, also read out a report on the question of the Russian refugees, while the matter of nominating a High Commissioner was discussed. The High Commissioner's first duty would be to find a practical solution to the problem of the Russian refugees. It was understood that his work did not simply consist of bringing material aid to the refugees in distress, but rather to assure the coordination of the efforts made by other organizations already working in their favour. It was suggested that the chairman himself might proceed with such a nomination with the approval of his colleagues. However, the Council instructed the Secretary-General to send out a questionnaire to the member states of the League. The numerous replies which were received emphasized the need for the coordination of the efforts and the centralization of action on behalf of Russian refugees. [17]

Rather than restore their entitlement to Russian citizenship, in December 1921 the new Union of Soviet Socialist Republics (USSR) withdrew diplomatic recognition and protection from the Russian exiles scattered across Europe and the Far East. This had profound consequences on millions of people who, as an official of the League of Nations put it, "cannot work, marry, be born or die without creating legal problems to which there is no solution."

The matter came up again at the fourteenth session of the Council in June 1921. [18] Secretary-General Drummond issued a memorandum summing up the discussions regarding the Russian refugees. He sent to each member government of the League a circular asking them whether they considered themselves concerned by the problem of the Russian refugees, and whether they would attend a conference summoned by the Council to study the matter. The initial response was encouraging. After cautiously affirmative answers to the Council's enquiry, member states resolved to appoint a High Commissioner for Russian Refugees. The conference started in Geneva on 22 August 1921 and lasted four days. They decided to appoint a High Commissioner for the purpose of reaching "a definite settlement of the refugee question." After reviewing the various aspects of the problem, the delegates adopted eleven resolutions on points which they wished to draw to the attention of a future High Commissioner, who would enter upon his duties immediately. The eleventh one reads: "In view of the close connection between the question of relief work proposed by the powers in favour of the starving populations and the question of Russian refugees abroad, the conference considers it would be desirable to coordinate the two activities." The League nominated Nansen as the High Commissioner. [19]

Nansen, who was in Moscow negotiating famine relief, was duly informed by telegram on the following day, 23 August. Once again, Nansen accepted the task, despite the complexity of the situation and despite his other on-going activities. It was clear that the matters of repatriating prisoners-of-war and feeding the starving populations were not entirely over, but Nansen's involvement had diminished. Nansen intended to arrive in Geneva at the beginning of September 1921 and it was hoped that he would begin work immediately.

Nansen was already thinking about taking on this responsibility beforehand. He saw the refugee crisis, the Russian famine and the repatriation of prisoners-of-war as interconnected. Noel-Baker, Frick and others had pressured Nansen to become high commissioner for refugees in June, but at that time he was not ready to undertake it. It was the declaration of the famine that convinced him to take on all three duties. They were all part of what in those days was called "the Russian question."

WORK BEGINS ON THE REFUGEE CRISIS

The first step Nansen took in September 1921 was to invite the voluntary organizations to form a joint committee to give him the benefit of their experience in handling the problem of Russian refugees. Government representatives were appointed to keep in touch with the High Commissioner and he also appointed his own representatives in each country concerned. As his deputies, Nansen appointed the multilingual Édouard Frick and the extraordinarily resourceful Philip Noel-Baker. His personal secretary was Major T.F. Johnson, a former British army officer, who manned the office in Geneva.

The position was indeed serious. The Russian refugees were to a large extent the legacy of the Russian Revolution of 1917. The tide had begun changing inside the fracturing Russian Empire in 1918 with the opening stages of the Civil War. It was estimated that there were by now between 1.5 and 2 million refugees scattered in countries stretching from France to China.

The Baltic republics, the Balkan monarchies and Poland—all very precarious states—contemplated with alarm the spectacle of tens of thousands of destitute Russians pouring across their brand new frontiers. In short, it was just the sort of international emergency calculated to test the willingness of member states to keep the promises made in setting up the League of Nations at Versailles.

There seemed to be three obvious ways of tackling the refugee problem: (a) the refugees should be returned to where they came from; (b) they should be transported to and settled in another country that would welcome them; and (c) they should be assimilated into the country where they were already located. On 22 March 1922 Nansen declared to the Council of the League of Nations: "In the long run, there can be no final and satisfactory solution [...] except by their repatriation to their native land." This attitude was to prove mistaken, since many refugee organizations were of the opinion that return-ees faced political persecution or worse if they went back to Soviet Russia. Although people were thinking along these lines, the famine situation made repatriation unthinkable in the spring of 1922. For instance, the French dele-gate to the League of Nations, Léon Bourgois, wrote the following in a letter to Nansen (in French). [20]

> The French Government has already made great efforts to return the greatest possible number of Russians to Russia. It has encountered difficulties due to the scarcity of transport in France and the distances involved. It will be easy to ascertain by examining the notes that, from our side, everything possible has been done. One ought also to stress that from the Soviet side it is not always easy to find a solution. Thus, the rules of priorities fixed by the Copenhagen Agreement of this current 20th April for the return of the French detained in Russia have not been thoroughly observed.

Nevertheless, by July 1922 Nansen had opened negotiations in Berlin with a Soviet representative, Nikolai Krestinsky, about repatriating a first batch of refugees. There were two serious doubts: first about the refugees' safety and secondly about their willingness to return. Nansen announced that a public amnesty of 21 November 1921 would apply to all who returned. Further-more, he would appoint representatives in Russia who would have the oppor-tunity to monitor the returnees' well-being, including guarantees for their safety verified by his own agents. Gustav Ador of the Red Cross denounced these guarantees as worthless, since he believed that many of the refugees were likely to be arrested, imprisoned and executed. In October 1922 a small group of Russian refugees were successfully transferred from Bulgaria to the Don and Kuban regions of Russia through the agency of the Soviet Red Cross. Fatefully, once they had arrived at their destination, the High Com-missioner could do nothing to guarantee their safety.

Within a few months the Russian emigrant press began reporting that some of the returnees had been shot by the Soviet authorities. The High Commissioner's office investigated the matter in the summer of 1923 and found that a number of former White Army officers had disappeared, while other refugees had been arrested. Clearly, the Soviet government had no intention of respecting the amnesty and the refugees had every reason to be apprehensive about returning home. In November 1923 Nansen himself at-tempted to interview some named returnees at Rostov-on-Don—but nobody turned up. He observed rather artlessly: "It may be that they did not find me and went away again." Despite this alarming situation, there was increased pressure from Albania, France, Poland and Romania to send the refugees home. Nansen had to intervene personally to prevent Romania and Poland from throwing refugees out of the country.

Nansen's work on the Russian refugees had hardly been commenced before a difficult problem of special urgency arose in Constantinople. Wrangel's Army and its civilian protégés had been rescued from the Crimean beaches by a ramshackle fleet of rusting merchant ships. Wrangel had been commanding general of the anti-Bolshevik White Army in Southern Russia in the later stages of the Civil War. These people had been evacuated to camps at Constantinople and Gallipoli, which were desperately over-crowded; epidemics threatened. The Turks did not want them. Wrangel's group had, up to that time, been supported by the French Government and the American Red Cross. Suddenly, the French Government, hitherto the main source of financial support, announced that it would be forced to sever supplies—it wanted to cut its losses having backed the wrong horse in the Russian Civil War. Although Nansen disliked dealing with the conservative White Russian leaders, he persuaded the French to continue to feed the refugees until they could be evacuated elsewhere. He also appealed to other governments and to private organizations for help.

Concerning Wrangel's defeated army—with women and children alto-gether 90,000 souls—some 10,000 were permitted to enter Bulgaria. Of these 7,000 were later given permission to return to Russia. The Bulgarian Govern-ment became afraid of the spread of communism and, in the spring of 1925, began forcibly sending refugees back home without travel visas. Some 250 Russian refugees were launched across the Black Sea in the direction of Odessa on board a small fragile vessel with meagre provisions. However, there was no agreement to receive them at their destination. The Russian Government sent them back again across the Black Sea. Whither? They could not go to Russia or Bulgaria. There was nothing for it but to try Turkey. Almost out of food and water and with the ship was in danger of sinking, at last with great joy they reached Constantinople. But to their disap-pointment they were not allowed to land here either. A tug came out to tow the craft through the Bosporus and out into the Black Sea. Now there were panic on board, with many of the Russians leaping into the sea. An English steamer came to their rescue and the captain frightened the Turkish police into allowing the Russians to disembark. The refugees led a frightful exis-tence in their miserable camp in an enclosed area with nothing but bare ground. Death began to take its toll. It would have been the end for most of them had not Anna Mitchell at the League's office for refugees at Constan-tinople collected money from the American-European colony in the town—enough for a daily ration of a little bread and a cup of thin soup. This is where Nansen found them. By the time Nansen visited the camp on 9 June, Mitchell's funds were exhausted. The refugees' money, some 700 Turkish pounds, had been confiscated by the Turkish police. Nansen applied to the Russian Government which referred him to the Bulgarian Government. The Bulgarian Government would not take the refugees back, the Turkish

Government would not allow them to remain in Constantinople, and other countries also refused to accept them. The further significance of this was that Bulgaria could not be used for the transit of refugees coming from other countries.

On the day that Nansen visited the refugee camps in Constantinople, there was a military *coup d'état* in Bulgaria and the new government demanded the immediate expulsion of members of the Soviet Red Cross delegation, who were arrested on charges of spying and distributing propaganda. Litvinov asked Nansen to ensure that the Soviet Red Cross workers were given proper protection, but two of them died in custody. Following the events in Bulgaria, the Soviet Government lost interest in repatriations and, on 4 August 1923, the Russians stopped all further returns by refugees on the grounds that they contained "counter-revolutionary elements."

Nansen now used a sum of money placed at his disposal by the publisher Christian Erichsen of Copenhagen to arrange for the temporary maintenance of the refugees. Subsequently, the large American Near-East Relief organization supported them for a couple of months on condition that a definitive settlement could be guaranteed within that time. Nansen then induced France to take a number of them "who were good workers" and the Soviet Government in Moscow took the rest "on condition that the Bulgarians abstain in the future from sending Russian refugees to Russia without making the necessary arrangements with Moscow."[21]

Despite these prodigious efforts, on 27 August 1923 *The Times* of London requested Nansen to resign as High Commissioner since it felt that he had a conflict of interest between refugee work and famine relief. He was accused of having better relations with the Soviet Government than with the various refugee organizations. He had set up two model farms in the Volga region and the Ukraine and it was said that he was benefiting financially from this arrangement. An unimpressed British member of parliament, Sir Samuel Hoare, said that it was a mistake to give the responsibility of famine relief and refugees to the same person.

If repatriation was not going to work, then the next alternative was to integrate the refugees into the country where they were located—a daunting task. Governments had to be approached to find homes for the refugees, transport had to be arranged and all the time food supplied.

If the refugees could not return to Russia and could not be absorbed into the country of refuge, then host countries had to be found, and work too in countries already deeply affected by the global economic crisis and high unemployment. The refugees often lived precariously and could find no haven or employment, being shunted around from one country to another. The lucky ones were transported in small groups to countries where employment opportunities existed in Central or Western Europe, and particularly to France. In *The Saga of Fridtjof Nansen* by Jon Sorensen we can read:

In Poland, there were altogether too many refugees. A decree was issued stating that all who had crossed the border illegally from Russia and who were not political refugees must leave the country before a certain day. They were Russian Jews, all these refugees, and there were many thousands of them. Back to Russia they could not go—they would be shot. There were driven across the border to Danzig but could not remain there. Thus they were driven across the borders again, and so these poor people were tossed like a tennis ball.

At Nansen's suggestion, the European Jews, through their organization in Paris, undertook to maintain them until an arrangement could be made. Several thousand refugees assembled in the camp outside Danzig until they were finally sent to the United States.

When discussing the refugee situation in Constantinople, one has also to bear in mind that, with the breakdown of the Treaty of Sèvres and the dismantling of the whole Ottoman Empire, huge numbers of Greek, Turkish and Armenian refugees were also flowing through this part of the world. After the city had been occupied by the Allies in 1920, Constantinople became an asylum for refugees, a haven on their flight from country to country, where at least they were temporarily safe. Throughout the centuries, Constantinople had seen many tragedies but hardly such an accumulation of human misery as there was when wave after wave of refugees washed up in the city—first the Russians, then the Turks, the Armenians and finally the Greeks.

About 170,000 Russians, 75,000 Turks and 155,000 Greeks and Armenians give some idea of the magnitude of the refugee problem confronting the relief activities of the League of Nations and other organizations in Constantinople. From September 1922 to September 1923, the League of Nations was able to send 20,000 refugees from Constantinople to forty-five different countries and the following year 6,000 refugees.

Nansen succeeded in placing thousands of children and students in Czechoslovakia. Bulgaria, which now accepted thousands of adult refugees, also took 5,000 children and put them in Russian-speaking schools. Bulgaria also took 1,000 disabled men with families. A large number of Jews were settled in Palestine and in the United States. The British Government, which had spent enormous sums on maintaining the refugees, voted £150,000 sterling on condition that Nansen would assume all future responsibility and that any possible surplus be divided equally between the British Government and Nansen's relief work. Nansen handled the transport of the refugees in three weeks for £70,000; thus, according to the arrangement with the British Government, he gained £40,000, a welcome addition to the funds for helping other refugees.

Nansen was always concerned that children and young people should receive education. He proposed that all the governments belonging to the League of Nations should accept Russian students and maintain them at universities. Czechoslovakia and France responded first and set a good example. It was, in his opinion, clear that the future depended on the acquisition of skills by the growing generation.[22]

HOW MANY REFUGEES?

How many people actually fled from Russia? A precise figure can never be known, for even approximate estimates vary widely and no single source could be trusted above the others. One fact was sure: nobody knew for certain how many refugees were in any country at any moment. Private relief agencies saw only a part of the refugee flood, while Nansen's own office depended on figures provided by individual governments for its statistics. These did not tell the whole story.[23]

The estimates of the number of Russian refugees who reached France ranged wildly from 60,000 to 400,000. The statistical data is most abundant and contradictory during the period 1919 to 1923, when the refugees were most mobile. This constant flux made it difficult for national authorities to keep a track of who lived where. It was not until 1926 that national origin was included on the French census form as a question to be answered by foreign-born respondents. Until then, therefore, bureaucratic estimates of the number of Russians in France were only marginally more trustworthy that the figures offered for Eastern Europe, the Middle East or China.

Early in 1922, the orientalist Vasily Nikitin offered a detailed analysis of the political affiliations of émigrés for the readers of the *La Revue des sciences politiques*. He declared that all political classes were represented, with the pre-revolutionary privileged classes not much more than a quarter of the whole.

In the autumn of 1921 another conference took place in Geneva during the annual meeting of the League's Assembly with the aim of reviewing the refugee problem from a more technical point of view. In order to prepare for the eventual establishment of refugees in countries where they would find employment it was necessary to obtain some information about them. The assistance of the ILO was requested for this aspect of the problem. The participants instructed the High Commissioner to carry out a general enquiry in collaboration with the ILO into the number of refugees, their professions, etc. Nansen organized a census in order to ascertain not only the numbers but also what work the refugees were capable of undertaking. Next, host governments had to be approached to find out what types of refugees they were prepared to receive and how many. Owing to the general economic situation at the time the responses were rather disappointing, but Nansen persisted in pressing for help and gradually more promises to accept refugees arrived.

The basis of subsequent international refugee law was established through legal developments during Nansen's tenure as High Commissioner. The most remarkable of these developments was the so-called Nansen Passport, which accorded certain rights to stateless refugees who did not possess any identity documents.

NOTES

1. MacMillan, M. *Paris 1919: Six months that changed the world*, pp. 69–70. New York, NY: Random House Paperbacks, 2001.

2. United States of America, Department of State. *Foreign Relations of the United States, Paris Peace Conference 1919*, volume III, p. 581. Washington, DC: Government Printing Office, 1943.

3. Ibid.

4. MacMillan, p. 18–63.

5. Nansen and Hoover's previous attempts to provide relief to Russia in 1919 have already been discussed in Chapter II.

6. Whittaker, D.J. *Fighter for Peace: Philip Noel-Baker, 1889–1982,* p. 51. York, UK: William Sessions Ltd., 1989.

7. Records of the Second Assembly of the League of Nations. Plenary Meetings. 1921.

8. The Sixth Committee dealt with political and minority issues, such as the admission of new states, mandates, minority issues and political disputes.

9. Whittaker, p. 51.

10. For letters and petitions against Nansen, see Nansen Funds, League of Nations Archives.

11. Whittaker, p. 182.

12. Fisher, H.H. *Famine in Soviet Russia 1919–1923: The Operations of the American Relief Administration.* New York, NY: The Macmillan Company, 1927.

13. Ibid.

14. Huntford, R. *Nansen: The Explorer as Hero,* p. 625. London: Abacus, 1997.

15. Minutes of thirteenth session of the Council of the League of Nations, League of Nations Archives.

16. Letter dated 15 June 1921, from the International Red Cross, presented to the thirteenth session of the Council of the League of Nations, Minutes of the Council, pp. 53-54, and in annex 224a.

17. Minutes of the thirteenth session of the Council of the League of Nations, pp. 54-54, and Annex 224 and 224a, League of Nations Archives. Also confirmed in the Report from the Fifth Committee presented to the third Assembly of the League of Nations, September 1922

18. Minutes of fourteenth session of the Council of the League of Nations, League of Nations Archives.

19. Ibid., p. 65

20. Letter from Léon Bourgeois to Nansen, 13 June 1920, Nansen Funds, ref. 40/4889/2792, box R–1755, League of Nations Archives.

21. Sorensen, J. *The Saga of Fridtjof Nansen,* p. 283. London: George Allen & Unwin, 1932.

22. Ibid., p. 286.

23. Johnston, R.H. *New Mecca New Babylon: Paris and the Russian Exiles, 1920–1945,* pp. 12–20. Montreal, Canada: McGill-Queen's University Press, 1988.

Nansen as a young man.

Nansen as an explorer.

Nansen as an international public figure.

Nansen as an old man.

The Norwegian Delegation at the second Assembly of the League of Nations, 1921. Members of the delegation were: Dr Fridtjof Nansen, M.O. Blehr (Prime Minister), Christian Michelet (Member of Parliament and former Minister of Foreign Affairs), Dr Christian Lange, Dr Michael H. Lie, Dr Kristine Bonnevie, Jens Bull, Toralv Oeksnevad and Jacob Jorstad.

The Right Hon Sir J. RENNEL RODD

M. P. BAKER
Secrétaire adjoint

Cartoon of Philip Noel-Baker by Derso and Kelen. Noel-Baker was Sir Eric Drummond's private secretary, and became Nansen's close collaborator assisting him in the repatriation and refugee work. [Archives of the League of Nations, Geneva.]

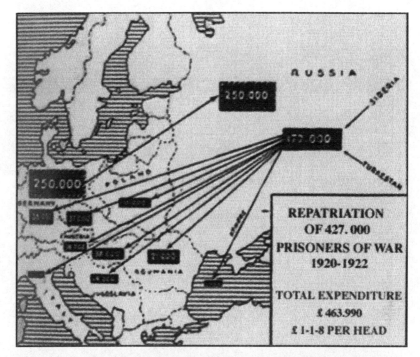

A map showing the repatriation of 427,000 prisoners of war from the First World War between 1920 and 1922 who had been interned in Germany and the former Russian Empire. [Illustration appearing in Essential Facts about the League of Nations, 1939.]

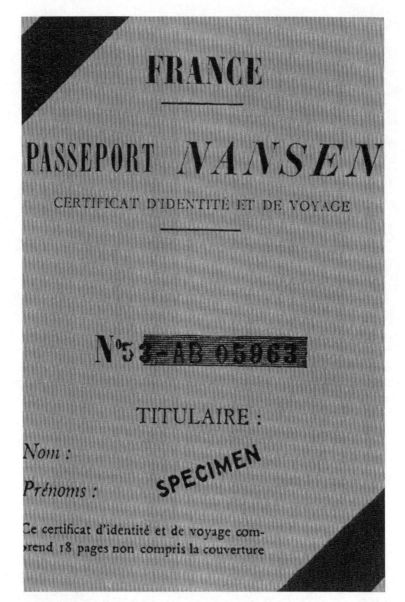

A specimen Nansen passport (for France). On 5 July 1922 an international agreement was concluded in Geneva which launched the eponymous identity card for displaced persons.

Chapter Five

Massacres and Treaties in Asia Minor

After his responsibilities for prisoners-of-war, Russian refugees and famine relief, much of Nansen's activities during the 1920s were concerned with addressing the turmoil in the Near East and the Caucasus. It is necessary to explain the events resulting in deceived hopes, betrayed promises and flight which were the outcome for many peoples in the Caucasus, the Eastern Mediterranean, Arabia, Mesopotamia and the Asia Minor following the First World War.

THE TREATY OF SÈVRES

The decision of the Ottoman Government to seek an immediate end to hostilities with the Allies followed the collapse of Bulgaria in the middle of September 1918. For nearly three years the Bulgarian and German Armies had held off the Allied Expeditionary Force centred on Salonika, but their front was finally broken by French, British, Serbian and Greek troops commanded by the French general Louis Franchet d'Esperey.

At the Paris Peace Conference of 1919, friction quickly developed between the Great Powers over middle-Eastern affairs. The armistice that had been signed with Turkey on 30 October 1918 led to a bitter quarrel between the British and the French, intensifying France's distrust about British intentions in the Near East. [1]

At the beginning of the Peace Conference there seemed to be a fair amount of agreement among the Great Powers on the basic issues. For instance, all parties appeared ready to exclude the Turks from Europe and to establish international control over the Dardanelles and the Bosporus. All agreed that some form of self-determination should be granted to the Arab peoples of the former Ottoman Empire. Without any precise definition of frontiers, negotiations conducted with the Emir of Mecca had envisaged the independence of some Arab countries. All were in accord with the creation of an Armenian State. However, the Great Powers had different agendas for the Ottoman Empire and deciding on its fate turned out to be a very thorny issue. The fate of the "sick" Ottoman Empire had been subject of European diplomatic negotiations for much of the nineteenth century and the Allied Powers had drawn up further agreements during the course of the war. The best known are the Sykes-Picot Agreement of 1916 and the Balfour Declaration of 1917, but there were others. [2] The Sykes-Picot Agreement had contemplated a special region for Palestine and the Holy Places. In the Balfour Declaration of 2 November 1917, the British Government had undertaken to look favourably on the establishment a national home for the Jewish people in Palestine. All four of the Great Powers accepted the Balfour Declaration. It would seem that it only remained to settle the details, but these details were to prove problematic.

The principal aims of the British Government, strongly supported by its overseas dominions, were the destruction of the German Navy and the requisition of all its colonies. The top priority for France was what to do about Europe. The war had been fought primarily on French soil, resulting in widespread damage to the French economy and infrastructure; the French wanted revenge. As a result, the Near-East problems occupied less time, energy and manpower at the Quai d'Orsay.

Territorially, the French claimed Syria, Cilicia (the south-east coast of Anatolia), Lebanon and Palestine. They based their claims not only on historical rights but on Allied wartime commitments. The French argued that the 1916 Sykes-Picot Agreement, dividing the Arab provinces outside the Arabian Peninsula into areas of British and French control, must remain in force until a new arrangement was made. With regard to the non-Turkish parts of the Ottoman Empire, it was considered by the Allies that these peoples were not ready for self-government and to determine their own destinies.

One of the most formidable lobbies at the Peace Conference was the Greek delegation, headed by their charismatic Prime Minister Eleftherios Venizelos. Venizelos created a great impression in Paris, even among those delegates who bitterly opposed him. When General Smuts wrote his preliminary draft covenant for the League of Nations, he suggested that there should be a Commissioner—a kind of world governor, a man like Venizelos—to lead the future organization. However, in the course of the discussion the power given to the future Secretary-General of the League was much reduced. [3]

Venizelos had extraordinary ambitions about the future role of Greece in the Near East. [4] There was a concept of establishing a Greek state that would encompass all areas where there were large Greek populations such as in Thrace and along the shores of the Aegean and the Black Seas. The Treaty of

Neuilly with Bulgaria and the Treaty of Sèvres with the Ottoman Empire were triumphs both for Venizelos and for Greece. As the result of these treaties, Greece acquired Western Thrace, Eastern Thrace, Smyrna, the islands of Imvros and Tenedos at the entrance of the Dardanelles, and all of the Dodecanese islands except Rhodes. Digesting all these gains was to give Greece a bad attack of colic.

Other lobbying groups—Armenians, Syrians, Zionists, Georgians, Arabs—were very active during the Peace Conference with energetic demands for future independent states at the expense of the former Ottoman Empire. A British request that Kurdistan to be added to the draft resolution was readily accepted.

The British had realised that, during the First World War, "the Allied cause floated to victory on a wave of oil." Whereas Clemenceau's attitude was: "When I want some oil, I'll find it at my grocer's." The greatest oil field in the world existed in Mesopotamia and extended all the way up to Mosul in northern Iraq. The British persuaded the French to accept Syria in return for Mosul, but this left northern Iraq exposed to sudden attack from the north. It was for this reason that the British hoped to create an independent Kurdish state as a buffer zone between Armenia and the oil-rich provinces of Mesopotamia.[5]

On the other hand, with their economy in ruins the general attitude among the Turks was one of despair. It was only in June 1919 that the Ottoman Delegation was allowed to speak to the Supreme Council in Paris.[6] From July to November 1919, the Peace Conference put aside the problem of the Ottoman Empire. The Europeans had agreed that there was little that could be done until the United States' position on mandates was known, and therefore they concentrated their efforts on other pressing issues. The twelfth of President Wilson's Fourteen Points stated: "The Turkish positions of the present Ottoman Empire should be assured a secure sovereignty, but the other nationalities which now are under Turkish rule should be assured an undoubted security of life and . . . autonomous development."

It was believed most appropriate that the administration of these former Ottoman territories should be placed in the hands of the League of Nations. A major decision was the creation of a system of mandates to be administered by the League of Nations in the Near East. Such an arrangement actually named the territories to be separated from the Ottoman Empire, with the result that the terms of the Sykes-Picot Agreement were no longer valid. The British saw it as a means of gaining unfettered jurisdiction over Palestine, as well as a possible way out of the moral dilemma resulting from conflicting French, Jewish and Arab claims. Clemenceau did not seem to understand that mandates deprived France of its ambitions to annex Syria. The French would, however, receive the League mandate to govern Syria.

In November 1919 it became clear that the United States would not accept any mandatory power, and therefore it became important for the British
and French to reach agreement over zones of influence in Asia Minor and the
Near East. The discussions started in December in London. The Allies were
in fact worried about the rising power of the Turkish Nationalist Movement
under Mustafa Kemal. The discussions would take place in London, while
the signing of the peace treaty with the Turkish delegation would take place
in Paris.[7]

The Conference of London convened between February and April 1920.
It implemented most of the decisions already made between the French and
the British, and initiated new pronouncements relating to Smyrna, financial
control and economic spheres of influence. It dealt with a wide variety of
non-Turkish problems, such as the Greek and Armenian questions also affecting a new Turkish state.[8] By the time the Conference closed, a draft
treaty had been adopted awaiting final approval from the Supreme Council
that would be meeting in San Remo in April 1920.[9]

The Treaty of Sèvres was drawn up between the Ottoman Empire and the
Allies—the Allies more or less dictating their terms to the "puppet" Ottoman
Government. The Allies seemed to be in a position to carve up Anatolia with
total impunity, but it was a shock to the world that they agreed to maintain
the defunct Ottoman Government in Constantinople. Large parts of the east
of the country were promised to the Armenians and Kurds, while even larger
parts were declared to be under the jurisdiction of Italy, France and the
United Kingdom. On 10 August 1920 at Sèvres near Paris the Turkish treaty
and five other separate treaties or agreements were signed concerning
Thrace, Greece, Armenia and the Aegean Islands. The long struggle to create
a Turkish treaty was at an end—or so the participants thought. It did not take
long before the Allies realised that it was not going to work. The Greek
invasion of Anatolia failed and the Kemalist forces regained the offensive.

By the spring 1922, the Allies were seeking to revise the treaty, while a
total Kemalist military victory in the summer if 1923 resulted in an entirely
new situation. The Treaty of Sèvres turned out to be null and void. It had
been signed by the Ottoman Government in Constantinople, whereas most
Turks recognized the authority of the government in Ankara headed by Mustafa Kemal. They feared with some justification that their country was being
shared out in the manner of the European colonial empires without any
consideration for the desires of the Turkish people. At the same time the
Syrian population resented French rule; the Turks around Mosul were attacking the British; the Arabs were in arms against the British rule in Baghdad;
there was also disorder in Egypt.

Earlier, the Turkish Nationalist Movement had signed the Amasya Agreement in 1919, which would result in the creation of a new government and
the setting up of a Turkish Grand National Assembly in Ankara. Not surpris-

ingly, a wave of indignation swept the Assembly when it learned that the Ottoman sultan had signed the Treaty of Sèvres. The new Turkish Government rejected the treaty and declared that henceforth the only source of political decision-making for the Turkish people would be the Grand National Assembly.

When establishing the Treaty of Sèvres, France, Italy and the United Kingdom had also entered into a secret "tripartite agreement." This agreement confirmed the United Kingdom's oil and commercial concessions in the Middle East and turned the former German enterprises in the Ottoman Empire over to a tripartite corporation.

The United States decided to have nothing to do with the partition of the Ottoman Empire. Russia was also excluded from these treaties because it had already negotiated the Treaty of Brest-Litovsk with the Ottoman Empire in 1918. In that treaty, the Ottoman Government had regained all of the lands Russia had captured in the First World War and in the previous Russo-Turkish War (1877–1878).

The Treaty of Lausanne of 24 July 1923 was the only First World War Peace Treaty that was truly negotiated between the victors and the vanquished. This treaty constituted an overwhelming diplomatic victory for the Turkish Nationalist movement.

THE ESTABLISHMENT OF THE MANDATES SYSTEM

In the plan for a League of Nations, published by General Smuts in December 1918 on the eve of the Conference of Peace, we find for the first time the broad outlines of an international mandates system. The author described in twenty-one points, each accompanied by a commentary, the main characteristics of what, in his view, what the future international organization should look like. The first nine points related to the fate of countries which had belonged to the European or Near-Eastern Empires which had collapsed. In respect to these territories General Smuts proposed that the League of Nations should be regarded as having "the right of ultimate disposal in accordance with the fundamental principles," in other words the League would have the last word. [10]

In their capacity as the victors of the First World War, France and the United Kingdom had intended simply to annex a number of these countries. However, Smuts feared that there would be an undignified "scramble among the victors for this loot" and suggests instead: "Reversion to the League of Nations should be substituted for any policy of national annexation." This meant that the right to intervene in the government of these countries would only be authorized by the League. On the other hand, the peoples of these countries were hoping that the principle of self-determination would be applied to them. Nevertheless, the ability of these territories to govern themselves varied considerably from one country to another. For some of them, General Smuts continues, "it will be found that they are as yet deficient in the qualities of statehood and that . . . they will in one degree or another require the guiding hand of some external authority to steady their administration." Smuts foresees other cases where "owing chiefly to the heterogeneous character of the population and their incapacity of administrative cooperation, autonomy in any real sense would be out of question and the administration would have to be undertaken to a very large extent by some external authority." In any case, this would be true of Palestine. "No State," continues General Smuts, "should make use of the helpless or weak condition of any of these territories in order to exploit them for its own purposes." All of these considerations are summed up by General Smuts in the following recommendation:

> (4) That any authority, control, or administration which may be necessary in respect of these territories and peoples, other than their own self-determination autonomy, shall be the exclusive function of and shall be vested in the League of Nations and exercised by or behalf of it. [11]

One question arises immediately: How is the League to impose this authority? The main body of the League would consist of a conference made up of national representatives. Any authority or administration would have an international character. The author goes on to indicate the weak points of an international administration: Up until this time, joint international administration had worked fairly well in limited situations such as for international postal arrangements. But when it has been tried in the government of peoples or territories, it had failed.

The administrative personnel taken from different nations did not work together well. The inhabitants of any territory administered in this way would either be confused or, if they were smart enough, would exploit the system by playing different nationals off against each other. In any case, the result would be "paralysis tempered by intrigue." Smuts asserted that if the League of Nations attempted to administer anything directly through its own personnel, it could easily turn into a fiasco. "The only successful administration of underdeveloped or subject people has been carried on by States with long experience for the purpose and staffs whose training and singleness of mind fit them for so difficult and special a task. . . . That is to say, where an autonomous people or territory requires a measure of administrative assistance, advice or control, the League should as a rule meet the case not by direct appointment of international officials but by nominating a particular State to act for and on behalf of it in the matter." [12] Thus, General Smuts recommends that, subject to the supervision and ultimate control of the

League, the mandate should be carried out by a designated state. Nevertheless, he points out:

> The delegation of certain powers to the mandatory States must not be looked up on as in any way impairing the ultimate authority and control of the League. . . . For this purpose it is important, that in each such case of mandate, the League should issue a special Act or Charter clearly setting forth the policy which the mandatory will have to follow in that territory. . . . The mandatory State should look upon its position as a great trust and honour, not as an office of profit or a position of private advantage for it or its nationals. [13]

Accordingly he recommends:

> (6) That the degree of authority, control or administration exercised by the mandatory State shall in each case be laid down by the League in a special Act or Charter, which shall reserve to it complete power of ultimate control and supervision, as well as the right of appeal to it from the territory or people affected against any gross breach of the mandate by the mandatory States
> (7) That the mandatory State shall in each case be bound to maintain the policy of the open door, or equal economic opportunity for all, and shall form no military forces beyond the standard laid down by the League for purposes of internal police. [14]

General Smuts' plan envisaged mandates only on the territories of Eastern Europe and of the Near East which would be decided by the Paris Peace Conference. As regards the German colonies, they were in the General's opinion "inhabited by barbarians who not only cannot possibly govern themselves but to whom it would be impracticable to apply any deals of political self-determination in the European sense. . . . The disposal of these colonies should be decided on the principles which President Wilson has laid down in the fifth of his celebrated Fourteen Points."

Despite their original intention to annex the former German and Ottoman territories and to share them out equally, France and the United Kingdom accepted the "mandates" system. However, according to Article 119 of the Treaty of Versailles, the German colonies in Africa and the Pacific were not handed over to the League of Nations, but to the Principal Allied and Associated Powers. Article 132 of the Treaty of Sèvres of 1920 contained a similar clause whereby Turkey renounced all rights over its territories outside Europe. As we already know, the Treaty of Sèvres never came into force and was replaced by the Treaty of Lausanne, which we shall come to in a minute. It was for the Supreme Council of the Allied Powers, and not the League of Nations, to select the countries that would have mandatory powers over these territories. On 7 May 1919 the system of mandates was introduced. The mandatories for Syria, Palestine and Mesopotamia (Iraq) were designated by the Supreme Council at San Remo on 25 April 1920. France was entrusted with the administration of Syria/Lebanon and the United Kingdom with that of Palestine/Transjordan and Iraq.

Although the League of Nations played no part in the designation of the mandatory powers, it did have supervisory powers granting "charters" to the selected mandatories. These charters specified the conditions for governing various countries.

According to Article 22 of the Covenant of the League of Nations: "the degree of authority, control or administration to be exercised by the Mandatory shall, if not previously agreed upon by the Members of the League, be explicitly defined in each case by the Council [of the League of Nations]." The interpretation and application of this clause was to going to cause problems. It would seem that the authors of the Covenant had at first intended to insert the precise terms of the mandates in the Peace Treaty, but this idea was subsequently dropped. In July 1919, a Committee composed of experts in colonial questions tried to establish the terms of mandates, but no agreement was reached because some of the governments concerned expressed reservations.

Subsequently, the Principal Allied and Associated Powers submitted to the League's Council a number of draft mandates which the latter adopted with slight amendments, after satisfying itself that they were in conformity with the terms of the Covenant. With regard, however, to the mandates for the Near Eastern territories (known as "A" mandates since they were expected to be short term before these countries achieved full independence), a considerable delay occurred mainly due to the intervention of the United States. In February 1921, the American Government asked to inspect the draft mandates. The Council, which before the receipt of this request had already postponed the subject, decided to comply with the wishes of Washington. In the course of the following eighteen months negotiations on the terms of these mandates took place between the United States and the various mandatory powers.

The two mandates for Palestine/Transjordan and for Syria/Lebanon were approved by the Council on 24 July 1922, subject to the outcome of negotiations between the French and the Italians. On 29 September 1923, France and Italy announced that agreement had been reached and the Council noted that the mandates for Syria/Lebanon and for Palestine/Transjordan would now enter into force.

The mandate for Iraq was delayed for several years. The Iraqi people, not unexpectedly, expressed a desire to have a national government of their own under an Arab ruler. The British Government, which had submitted a draft mandate to the Council in 1920, declared on 17 November 1921 that the political developments in Iraq called for a series of protocols and subsidiary agreements that were not ready until March 1924. The Council of the League of Nations finally approved the mandate for Iraq in 1926.

In order to supervise the working of the mandates system, the Council of the League of Nations created a Permanent Mandates Commission on 1 December 1920.

KURDISTAN, IRAQ, PALESTINE, AND SYRIA

A number of provisions in the Treaty of Sèvres had foreseen an independent territory for the Kurds. A Kurdish region was scheduled to have a referendum to decide its fate, which was to include the Mosul Province on the border between Turkey and Iraq. There was no general agreement among the Kurds on what their borders should be, because the areas of Kurdish settlement spread out across the existing international borders in the region and their population was mixed with Armenians and Turks. The outlines of a "Kurdistan" as an entity were proposed in 1919 by Şerif Pasha, who represented the Society for the Ascension of Kurdistan (Kürdistan Teali Cemiyeti) at the Paris Peace Conference. He defined the region's boundaries but caused controversy among other Kurdish nationalists themselves as it did not include the Van region (an area disputed with the Armenians). An alternative—one might say ambitious—map was proposed which included the city of Van and an improbable outlet to the sea via Turkey's present southern Hatay Province.

Neither of these proposals was endorsed by the Treaty of Sèvres, which suggested a much reduced Kurdistan located entirely on what is now Turkish territory. Finally, the Kurds received no offers for a separate territory from Iran, British-controlled Iraq and French-controlled Syria. However, even this reduced plan was never implemented because the Treaty of Sèvres was abandoned. Subsequently, in February 1925 a revolt broke out among the Kurds of eastern Anatolia. The revolt was suppressed by the Turks, the ringleaders hanged and some of the Kurdish population deported to central Anatolia.

The oil concession in this region was given to the British-controlled Turkish Petroleum Company (TPC) which had held rights to the Mosul province. With the elimination of the Ottoman Empire, British and Iraqi negotiators held acrimonious discussions over the new oil concession. However, the League of Nations had to vote on who would own Mosul and the Iraqis feared that, without British support, Mosul would be lost to Turkey. Finally, the League of Nations awarded Mosul to Iraq and the current Iraq-Turkish border was agreed in July 1926. In March 1925, the TPC, renamed the Iraq Petroleum Company (IPC), was granted a full concession for Mosul for a period of seventy-five years.

Palestine officially fell under the British Mandate granted by the League of Nations. The principles of the Balfour Declaration sent by the British

Foreign Secretary to Baron Rothschild (December 1917) regarding Palestine were incorporated into the Treaty of Sèvres:

ARTICLE 95.
The High Contracting Parties agree to entrust, by application of the provisions of Article 22, the administration of Palestine, within such boundaries as may be determined by the Principal Allied Powers, to a Mandatory to be selected by the said Powers. The Mandatory will be responsible for putting into effect the declaration originally made on November 2, 1917, by the British Government, and adopted by the other Allied Powers, in favour of the establishment in Palestine of a national home for the Jewish people, it being clearly understood that nothing shall be done which may prejudice the civil and religious rights of existing non-Jewish communities in Palestine, or the rights and political status enjoyed by Jews in any other country.

The French Mandate of Lebanon was agreed at the San Remo Conference. Syria was later assigned to France again under a League of Nations mandate. Faisal ibn Husayn, who had been proclaimed king of Syria by a Syrian national congress in Damascus in March 1920, was ejected by the French in July of the same year.

THE FATE OF THE ARMENIANS

In the winter of 1914–1915 the Turks had undertaken a disastrous military campaign in the Caucasus against the Russians resulting in the loss of the Turkish Ninth Army with its 40,000 men. In eastern Anatolia, the Armenian population numbered as much as 30% of the population and at the outbreak of the war they had shown little enthusiasm for the Turkish cause. This lukewarm attitude aroused the animosity of the Turks, although there were Armenian soldiers serving in the Turkish Army. During the Caucasus campaign the Armenians had spread confusion behind the Turkish lines by cutting communications and forming volunteer battalions which assisted the Russians, thus contributing to the Turkish debacle. This did not endear them to the Ottoman Government, which decided to deport "the accursed race" from eastern Anatolia. On the night of 24/25 April 1915 some 250 Armenian community leaders in Constantinople, including politicians, priests, doctors, authors, journalists, lawyers and teachers, were arrested. These mass arrests in Constantinople are considered as the start of the Armenian Genocide. During June and July 1915 men, women and children were rounded up and driven out of the country—deportation became a synonym for extermination. As the columns of refugees passed, foodless and destitute of all possessions, they were brutally attacked by the Turkish soldiers. Thousands died of burning, drowning, poison, forcible drug overdoses and inoculation with typhus. In some places wholesale massacres occurred. It has estimated that the Armenian population of the Ottoman Empire numbered 2 million in 1913; by 1920 fewer than 100,000 remained. A telegram dated 15 September 1915, and signed by Tala'at—Ottoman Minister of the Interior—concludes: "Regardless of women, children or invalids, and however deplorable the methods of destruction may seem, an end is to be put to their existence without paying any heed to feeling or conscience." A month previously Tala'at assured the German Government disingenuously that the Armenian problem no longer existed. Despite protests from the Germans and from the American ambassador, the slaughter went on.

Although Armenian history stretches back for many thousands of years, for 500 years before the twentieth century there had been no such thing as an Armenian State. Armenia was a geographic term referring to a people living on a territory spread out across the Ottoman Empire, Persia and southern Russia.

The history of Armenians between 1915 and 1922 is marked by a series of dramatic events, of which the genocide is the first. In 1918 Armenians unilaterally proclaimed the first Armenian Republic and fixed their capital at Yerevan on land that previously formed part of Tsarist Russia. There were about 1 million Armenians already living in the area and they were eventually joined by some 300,000 Armenian refugees. On 22 April 1918 a Trans-Caucasian Federal Republic was formed by Armenia, Azerbaijan and Georgia. A month later the federation broke up into three independent republics as they squabbled over their borders. The Armenians gained a great victory over the Turks in the battle of Sardarabad (modern-day Armavir) in May 1918. Sardarabad was only forty kilometres west of the city of Yerevan and the victory was seen as preventing the complete destruction of the Armenian nation.

The idea of the United Kingdom and France had been to create a single, large Armenian state uniting the population and located somewhere on the border between Turkish and Russian territory with its frontiers guaranteed by the United States. By the Treaty of Sèvres, Armenia was recognized as a free, independent and sovereign state and the American President Wilson was asked to establish the boundary between Turkey and Armenia. This border granted to Armenia what is today a large part of north-east Turkey. But both the treaty and Wilson's borders remained null and void. The annulment of the treaty meant that Armenia was once more likely to be threatened by Russia and Turkey who wanted to reclaim territory that they believed belonged to them. Following the Armistice of 1918 the Armenians had been able to establish their claim to this territory, but the victorious Allies did nothing to help them hang on to it. Nansen, with unusual cynicism, remarked: "There were no oil wells."

The Armenian Republic lasted for two years, until 1920, when its fate was decided by armed force. The country was finally overwhelmed by Mustafa Kemal's Turkish Nationalist Government and Russia. At the end of September 1920 both the Turkish Army and the Red Army advanced on the country. On 2 December 1920 Armenia signed a treaty with Turkey at Alexandropol which cancelled all their territorial ambitions in north-eastern Turkey. A year later the Treaty of Kars signed on 13 October 1921 was a "friendship" treaty and ratified in Yerevan on 11 September 1922. Signatories included representatives from the Grand National Assembly of Turkey and the future Soviet Armenia, Soviet Azerbaijan and Soviet Georgia. The treaty established the borders between Turkey and the South Caucasus states, particularly on and to the detriment of Armenian lands.

The Armenians' problems were far from over. By the end of December 1920 a Soviet communist government was installed in Armenia. In March 1922, Armenia, Azerbaijan and Georgia had once again been obliged to join a Trans-Caucasian Soviet Federated Socialist Republic, which became part of the USSR. The Treaty of Lausanne did nothing to save the Armenians. It was finally in 1936 that Armenia became an independent constituent republic of the USSR. Over fifty years later, on 23 August 1990, Armenia declared its independence, becoming the first non-Baltic republic to secede from the USSR.

It has been estimated that from the beginning of the First World War up to 1922, more than one-third of the Armenian race was exterminated. The persecution and atrocities meant that few people had any sympathy for the Turks. This inspired Nansen to find a homeland for the Armenians; in his obstinate opinion, the answer lay within Russia.

RESETTLING THE ARMENIANS

At the first annual Assembly of the League in 1920, Lord Robert Cecil had moved: "That the Council be requested to take into immediate consideration the situation in Armenia, and to present for the consideration of the Assembly proposals for averting the danger which now threatens the remnants of the Armenian race, and also for establishing a permanent settlement of that country."[15]

During these years, Nansen was also concerned with the Armenian problem. In support of Cecil's motion, Nansen went straight to the practical urgency of doing something about it. As he put it: "Before we can discuss the frontier question, it's necessary to save the people from destruction in order that there may be some people to occupy the country." He suggested that the League of Nations should organize a military expedition of 60,000 men to be sent at once to protect the Armenians from the Turks. Once more Nansen was ahead of his time by suggesting that the League of Nations should send an armed intervention force to protect a people under threat.

Finally, it was decided to appoint a Committee of Six to investigate the problem, with both Lord Robert Cecil and Nansen as members. They could do little more than urge upon the Council of the League of Nations the need for keeping an eye on Armenian affairs and seizing every opportunity for mediation.

At the second annual Assembly of the League (1921), Professor Gilbert Murray brought forward the case of Armenia again: "I venture to hope" he said, "that it will be the general wish of the Assembly that we do not part without having considered once more whether it is not possible to begin to discharge that debt which has been owed, not intended by the League of Nations, but by all Western Powers of Europe for so many years, and indeed for so many generations, to that much-suffering people."

The third Assembly (1922) once more urged the Council to take steps during the negotiations for peace with Turkey about providing a national home for the Armenians. During 1922 another large group of refugees came to join the half-million Armenians scattered throughout Europe and the Middle East—in Syria, Cyprus, Lebanon, Palestine, Greece and Bulgaria.

At last, the fourth Assembly (1923) took more direct action. The resolution adopted included the following:

> The Assembly: bearing in mind the resolutions passed by the first, second, and third ordinary sessions of the Assembly and by the Council in favour of the Armenians; Desirous of manifesting its sympathy towards these unfortunate people; Having considered the proposals made for the settlement of the Armenian refugees in the Caucasus and elsewhere; Considering it undesirable, however, to express any opinion on the merits of such proposals until they formed the subject of careful and impartial enquiries; Invites the International Labour Office, in collaboration with Dr Nansen, to institute an enquiry with a view to studying the possibility of settling a substantial number of Armenian refugees on the Caucasus or elsewhere.

While genocide in Asia Minor had led to the flight of the Armenians from Turkey, Nansen attempted to save the remnants of population from extinction. He drew up a political, industrial and financial plan for creating a national home for the Armenians. In a matter of weeks, thanks to the united efforts of private organizations and the League of Nations, the refugees were saved from famine and epidemics.

THE COMMISSION OF INQUIRY

From 1926 to 1929 Nansen spent a lot of time and effort on trying to settle Armenian refugees in Soviet Armenia. He had at first declined to undertake the new responsibility, but at length he consented to act in co-operation with the International Labour Organization (ILO). In fact, the proposal to settle

Armenian refugees in Soviet Armenia came from Albert Thomas, the energetic Director of the ILO. Thomas put together a Commission of Inquiry to
visit Armenia in 1925 and asked Nansen to head it. At first, the 64-year-old
Nansen refused because he was seriously thinking of retiring from humanitarian work. Thomas pointed out that the Soviet Government would not deal
with the League of Nations or any of its agencies, but would deal with
Nansen. Thus, Nansen accepted and travelled to Soviet Armenia with the
commission in the spring of 1925. He became fascinated by the land, the
culture and the people who almost lived in an earthly paradise, except for one
thing—water.

Nansen investigated the possibilities of organizing irrigation which would
allow the resettling of Armenian refugees on land situated to the east of
Yerevan. He worked in close co-operation with the Soviet committee for the
improvement of the land, but his requests for funds met with little response.
These setbacks affected him deeply. In 1927, overcome with melancholy and
depression, he tendered his resignation as High Commissioner for Refugees—but the League refused to accept it. Despite this failure, Nansen's
name is still revered among Armenians.

He reported the results of his trip to the League of Nations: "At this time
the only place where it is possible to settle Armenian refugees is Soviet
Armenia. Several years ago devastation, poverty and famine prevailed here,
yet now peace and order are established and the population even became
prosperous to some degree." Although the League failed to implement its
plan in general, Nansen still managed to resettle some refugees in Armenia,
as well as in Syria and Lebanon.

The commission submitted its report to the sixth Assembly of the League
of Nations in the autumn of 1925. The suggested scheme involved the drain-
age and irrigation of some 36,000 hectares of land in Armenia at a cost of
£900,000 enabling at least 15,000 more refugees to be settled. Nansen made
an eloquent appeal to the Assembly to undertake this comparatively modest
proposal. He concluded with these words:

> There is, in fact, in this little republic a national home for the Armenians at
> last, and I ask the members of the Assembly to put to their conscience the
> question whether they sincerely and earnestly believe that any other national
> home can be hoped for. I believe that I know the answer which their con-
> sciences will give and I appeal to the Assembly to approve this one effort to
> carry out all the promises which have been made in the past concerning a
> national home for the Armenian nation

Everyone hesitated to become involved because of previous bad experiences
with the Soviets. Ominously, the British Chancellor of the Exchequer was
Winston Churchill, a renowned anti-communist. His view was that, since the
USSR was moving towards control of the population through a rigid commu-

nist political system, it was not in the refugees' interest to settle them in Armenia: "It would be quite impossible to ask [the British] Parliament to vote money to turn Armenians into Communists." When he opposed the financing of irrigation in Armenia, the whole scheme collapsed. Attention now focused on resettling a large population of Armenians in Syria and Lebanon, at that time under French mandate. Many other Armenian refugees were able to spread out across the world: Bulgaria, Egypt, France, Hong Kong, Italy, Palestine, Poland, Romania, Singapore, Switzerland, Ukraine and the United States of America.

This did not seem to Nansen to be an adequate response to the Armenian people who had so often been promised that their country would be restored to them. Four years later, 100,000 of these refugees were allowed to settle in Soviet Armenia, in a barren area which would first have to be prepared for them. He continued to appeal for a loan similar to the one that the League of Nations had given to Greece, although the amount became less year by year. "I beg the members of each delegation to remind themselves of what the Armenian tragedy has been [...] the survivors of the Armenian nation are waiting for their help. I beg of them not to disappoint these people." He appealed to them in vain since his proposals continued to encounter the mistrust and hostility of governments. Neither the reports, which were favourable to the proposal, nor Nansen's renewed appeals succeeded in convincing the European governments to finance a loan. Even the Soviet Government lost interest in Nansen's irrigation schemes—if it ever had been.

The sixth Assembly (1925) of the League of Nations decided that it was desirable to send a further technical commission to examine the possibility of the irrigation plan. The latter worked in the country for six months and reported that the scheme was technically sound, but doubts were raised as to the possibility of raising the necessary loan on the guarantee of the Soviet State Bank. Nansen had hoped that the Western governments would, in view of their many previous expressions of interest in Armenia, themselves give the necessary guarantees. At the seventh Assembly (1926) he once more used all his powers of eloquence to persuade the governments to fulfil their promises to Armenia, now that there was a practicable scheme before them, approved and supported by experts.

> I beg them to think for a moment what the history of the Armenian people has been. During the past twelve months I have spent a great part of my time in studying the story of the Armenian people, and I have been forced to the conviction that no other people in recorded history have endured misery and maltreatment in any way comparable to that through which the Armenians have passed.

However, at the meeting of the Council of the League of Nations in June 1927, it became evident that it was Soviet Armenia itself that was making difficulties, particularly about accepting more refugees. When asked to set a quota, the reply from the Armenian authorities was vague. From this moment on it was obvious to everyone—except to Nansen—that Armenia could not and would not be helped.

NANSEN AND THE ARMENIANS

His trip to Armenia was described in the book *Gjennern Armenia* (Across Armenia), published in 1927. Two years later he also referred to the trip of 1925 in another book: *Gjennern Kaukasus til Volga* (Through the Caucasus to the Volga). Nansen continued to seek support for the Armenians until the end of his life. It was for this purpose that in 1928 he went to the United States of America giving a series of lectures to raise money for the Armenians. The financial outcome was meagre.

The full report of the Commission of Inquiry and other relevant papers were published by the League of Nations under the title *Scheme for the Settlement of Armenian Refugees* (Geneva, 1927). After returning to Norway Nansen wrote a more intimate account of the work in English under the title *Armenia and the Near East* (1928). It is a book full of sympathy and respect for the Armenian people, which was later published in Norwegian, French, German, Russian and Armenian.

Few responded to Nansen's appeal for the necessary money, considering it to be a hopeless "one-man show." Finally, at the tenth Assembly of the League of Nations (1929), Nansen, "his heart bleeding," was forced to take the question of a loan for the Armenian homeland off the agenda. Those measures of help given to Armenia came from private sources through the American Near-East Relief and other organizations. The tenth Assembly was the last one that Nansen attended.

Why did he spend so much time on this lost cause? Nansen had a very special interest in the small Republic of Armenia and had a very unusual relationship with the Soviet authorities, which was facilitated by his assistant Vidkun Quisling. There is no doubt that he admired the communist regime and believed that the Soviet authorities would eventually grant full internal sovereignty to Armenia. One reason for this attitude is that he felt that much of the early criticism of the USSR in the anti-communist press was exaggerated to the point of absurdity.

In contrast to his naïve confidence in the Soviet authorities, he never seems to have realised just how cynical and brutal they could be. Like many people, he may also have considered communism to be a transient phenomenon. Quisling, Nansen's agent in Moscow, had no illusions about the way the Bolsheviks ran the country. In 1927 he told Nansen that the "red terror" had begun: "Thousands of innocent citizens are arbitrarily arrested, exiled, shot or sent to overcrowded prisons." While up to 1929 Nansen continued to believe that sending refugees to Armenia was the ideal solution, Quisling realised that it would be an error. Finally, Nansen had to admit that the situation in the USSR was "less satisfactory" and many Armenians were actually trying to flee the campaign of terror. At last, he began to understand what other people had been saying since 1922—returning refugees were being executed.

Even though Nansen was not enthusiastic about it, a greater measure of success was achieved in Syria. Nansen considered Syria as a threat to his idea of a Republic of Armenia and continued to view the USSR as the land of opportunity. He believed that, since the Armenians were Christians, they were more likely to fit into the culture of Russia than into that of the Middle East. If Soviet Armenia was an artificial state constructed almost out of nothing, did it matter that Armenians should settle in Syria?

Some 90,000 Armenian refugees were gathered from the southern coastal region of Anatolia and transported to Syria after the French evacuated that country. Most of these refugees were in three overcrowded camps at Alexandretta, Aleppo and Beirut. The French appealed to the League for help in the work that they themselves and the voluntary organizations had been doing to cope with the situation. One of its worst aspects was the arrival of malaria in the camps and the menace of this spreading to surrounding districts.

A Joint Armenian Sub-Committee was appointed with Nansen as chairman. The first step was to get the refugees out of the temporary camps and into permanent housing. Urban and agricultural settlements were set up. By 1929 there were still 32,000 people in the camps which had at least been rendered sanitary, with clothes and food available. It was then hoped that, with the aid of the French and Lebanese Governments, it would be possible to carry out the scheme of re-settlement drawn up by the Committee.

NOTES

1. Helmreich, P. *From Paris to Sevres, the Partition of the Ottoman Empire at the Peace Conference of 1919–1920*, pp. 3–59. Columbus, OH: Ohio State University Press, 1974.

2. Among the other agreements were: the Constantinople Agreement of 1915; the Treaty of London of 1915; and the Saint Jean de Maurienne Agreement of 1917.

3. Barros, J. *An office without power: Secretary-General Sir Eric Drummond, 1919–33* , pp. 1–19. Oxford, UK: Oxford University Press, 1979.

4. Helmreich, pp. 38–46

5. Macmillan, M. *Paris 1919: Six Months that Changed the World,* p. 396. New York, NY: Random House, 2002.

6. US States Policy Papers, Paris Peace Conference 1919, vol. II, pp. 508–512, ref. 180.03110/69.

7. Helmreich, p. 223

8. Helmreich, pp. 265–87.

9. Helmreich, p. 290.

10. Smuts, J.C. *The League of Nations: A Practical Suggestion,* p. 12. London: Hodder & Stoughton, 1918.

11. Smuts, p. 17.

12. Smuts, p. 19 .

13. Smuts, p. 21.

14. Smuts, pp. 22–23.

15. Minutes of the first Assembly of the League of Nations.

Chapter Six

Trouble in Asia Minor

THE GREEKS OF SMYRNA

One of the most formidable petition groups at the Paris Peace Conference in 1919 was the Greek delegation, headed by Prime Minister Eleftherios Venizelos. At the beginning of the First World War, Greek politicians were divided as to whether they should support the Allies, the Central Powers or remain neutral. In 1915 the British Prime Minister Lloyd George tried to tempt Greece to join the Allies by promising territorial gains in Asia Minor. Greece had remained neutral throughout the early stages of the war, entering the fray only in June 1917 as a result of an anti-royalist rebellion.

This successful attack on the Greek monarchy had been led by Venizelos and supported both diplomatically and militarily by France and the United Kingdom. It is important to remember the overwhelmingly favourable impression created by Venizelos at the Paris Peace Conference. The Allied leaders felt a heavy debt of personal gratitude to Venizelos for his efforts in behalf of the Allied cause during the war.[1]

Thus it was that, according to the Treaty of Sèvres (10 August 1920), the Allied powers awarded Thrace to Greece as well as the district of Smyrna in Anatolia, which had a large Greek population. The British were also keen that the straights between the Black Sea and the Mediterranean should be permanently open to international shipping. Although the Ottomans controlled the Smyrna area, Greek influence had been strong in the city since the fourteenth century to the extent that the Turks called it "Smyrna of the Infidels." During the late nineteenth and early twentieth century, the city was an important financial and cultural centre of the Greek world.

According to the terms of the Treaty of Sèvres, in 1919 the Greek Army took possession of Smyrna, but had overestimated its ability to defend it.

Meanwhile, the Turkish Grand National Assembly in Ankara refused to ratify the Treaty of Sèvres and such was the reaction to it that a new and radical
Turkish independence movement arose led by Mustafa Kemal.

Smyrna would turn into a calamity. Terrible abuses were committed by
both sides. The Greek Army was poorly equipped and, due to the dismissal
of senior Greek officers for political reasons, was also poorly led. The British
and the French showed little support. While the United Kingdom favoured
the Greeks, the British Prime Minister did not want to upset Muslim nations
by showing too much enthusiasm. The French, on the other hand, wanted to
reach a compromise with the Turks. They even began to supply Turkey with
arms.

In March 1922, it was suggested that Greece and Turkey should sign an
armistice, but Mustafa Kemal demanded the total evacuation of Anatolia. By
September 1922, the situation was desperate. The Greek Army had been
ejected from Anatolia in disorder to the island of Chios, while their com-
mander-in-chief, General Trikupis, was captured. The Turks entered Smyrna
and began to massacre the Greek population, who fled in droves. Kemal
announced that Greeks would no longer be tolerated on Turkish soil. He then
began to march on Constantinople, where the French and British forces offered no resistance. Under these circumstances, the Allies were obliged to
enter into the long negotiations eventually leading to the Treaty of Lausanne.
Kemal's regime therefore began with a great military and political victory.
On the other hand, the Treaty of Lausanne would be disastrous for Greece. [2]

The Turkish authorities were not prepared to let the Greek and Armenian
refugees return to the Anatolian mainland. Nansen feared that, unless special
measures were taken to inspire the Christian populations of Constantinople
with more confidence for their future, there was a grave danger that a general
exodus would take place there as well. Indeed, the Turks had requested all
Greeks to leave Constantinople. Since the Greek population was the commercial and financial dynamo of the Near East, it was quite obvious that this
would bring about the ruin of the regional economy, and particularly that of
Constantinople. Eventually, the Turkish negotiators had to accept that the
Greeks would remain in the city, including their religious authorities. In
return, the Muslim population would be allowed to remain in eastern Thrace.

AN IDEA IS BORN

On 18 September 1922, Nansen addressed the following letter to the President of the Assembly of the League of Nations:

> Sir,
> I have received from my Assistant High Commissioner for Russian Refugees
> in Constantinople an urgent telegram requesting permission to utilize the or-

ganization of the High Commissariat in that city for administrating relief to the many thousands of Greek and Armenian refugees who have arrived there from Smyrna and Brousa.

As this request raises a question of principle of some importance, I venture to ask for your permission to lay the telegram before the Assembly at its next plenary meeting, and to suggest to the Assembly on what conditions I believe it might be complied with.

During the Assembly Nansen was asked to read out the telegram that he had received from his representative in Constantinople[3] which described the critical military situation in Smyrna and the resulting flow of refugees. Greek refugees had been obliged to flee their homes in Asia Minor after the defeat of the Greek Army. That same afternoon the matter was referred to and discussed by the Fifth Committee, where the Under-Secretary General, Bernardo Attolico, informed the members of the Committee that a sum of 300,000 Swiss francs existed under a credit allocated for "unforeseen expenditures," and he suggested that 100,000 francs of this money might be allocated to Nansen's appeal. Lord Balfour said that a great calamity had undoubtedly occurred and it was the League's duty to intervene. A month later the Assembly officially approved the sum of 100,000 Swiss francs to enable the necessary urgent administrative measures to be taken. The day following Nansen's presentation of the situation, the third Assembly recommended that "the High Commissioner of the League be authorised to utilise the services of the Russian Refugee organisations for administering the money collected for this purpose, it being understood that the League undertakes no responsibility for these refugees, that the work for the Russian refugees shall continue without hindrance and that this additional activity be considered of a temporary nature."

Thus, within twenty-four hours Nansen had persuaded the League to take action on his urgent appeal and the money was found within a month. The situation in Asia Minor required a tremendous amount of work and on 25 September Philip Noel-Baker described what had to be done.[4] He acknowledged that the League's had undertaken a new responsibility by organizing relief for the refugees of the Greek-Turkish War, and this responsibility would be exercised on behalf of the League by Nansen. He noted that the problem of refugees in Asia Minor could be broken down into three facets.

Constantinople
According to information at present available there are 120,000 refugees in Constantinople. They seem to be partly Greeks and partly Armenians and to come from the regions of Smyrna and Brousa . . .

Greece
According to information supplied to me by Dr Streit on 24 September 1922 there are about 400,000 refugees in Greece proper, a very great proportion of whom have arrived within the last two or three weeks from Asia Minor . . .

Smyrna
The problem of Smyrna is evidently much the most difficult. It is impossible to secure accurate figures. There are, however, certainly somewhere between 100,000 and 300,000 people who are not allowed by the Turks to leave either for abroad or for the interior of the country and to whom they will give nothing to eat. These people are already slowly starving to death and [it is] rumoured that the Turks intend to massacre them on the 30 [September] if they are still alive. In addition great number of Greeks of military age and of Armenians of all ages, are said to have been driven into the interior where they are being imprisoned and partly massacred. It seems urgently desirable that any steps which can be taken to restrain the excess of the Turks should be taken without delay. No doubt the most effective of all possible steps would be to send to Smyrna a representative of the League of Nations. If possible this representative should be a person of standing . . .

Noel-Baker then goes on to prepare a plan of action. He suggests that Nansen should demand the Assembly's permission to telegraph at once to Mustafa Kemal asking him to receive representatives of the League of Nations with a view to organizing relief for the refugees. Evidently, Kemal would be more motivated to react favourably if there was some money available for the purpose. Perhaps, he suggested, if the Greek Government would provide some financing, other governments would follow the lead of the United Kingdom in providing larger sums. If Kemal accepted the League's request for a meeting, Nansen should immediately proceed to Smyrna accompanied by the person whom he proposed to leave in charge there. The advantage of Noel-Baker's plan was that it would be very difficult for Mustafa Kemal to refuse such an invitation. His acceptance would be the best possible guarantee for the survival of the Christian populations and had the further political advantage of bringing the League into direct contact with Kemal. If he refused, it would considerably undermine his moral authority.

When Nansen made his statement about Smyrna to the Assembly and asked permission to telegraph Kemal on behalf of the League, he announced at the same time the possibility of money being made available by the Greek Government, and an offer by the British Government to contribute if the other members of the League were willing to do so. It would be easier for Nansen to use the British money at once if other countries proposed to make similar contributions soon afterwards. He also appealed to the whole world for contributions through such agencies as the American Near East Relief, the Lord Mayor's Fund, Colonel Procter's Committee, etc. Nansen announced how and where the money could be paid. Noel-Baker hoped that

Nansen's appeal would stimulate a considerable quantity of private charity and receive a quick response.

This episode clearly indicated what Nansen, the charismatic figurehead, could accomplish when conditions were in his favour. He had acted quickly and decisively outside the normal bureaucratic procedures. With the support of Balfour, Nansen's mandate had been considerably expanded to include a new group of refugees. The way in which this sudden emergency was faced not only illustrates his promptness in action but also the way that the field of refugee service was beginning to widen. There was now a precedent for taking charge of new groups of refugees resulting from an international emergency.

The Greek refugees presented a most difficult problem. By now, some 900,000 of them had arrived in Greece. Among them were at least some 50,000 Armenians to whom the Greek Government was distributing relief. A small country of some 5 million inhabitants was ultimately faced with absorbing about 1.5 million of its countrymen driven out of Asia Minor. The Greek Government had made every possible effort to spread these refugees throughout the country in such a way as to permit their absorption among the existing population, but many ended up living in squalor in temporary camps. The Turks were faced with a complementary problem; the departure of the Greek population of Smyrna resulted in vacant land and housing.

It occurred to Noel-Baker that if the Greeks expelled their Muslim minority, it would make room for the Greek refugees and provide the Turks with a new population for Smyrna. The first mention of this idea is in a letter from Noel-Baker to Secretary-General Drummond dated 9 October 1922. It is then repeated in a letter from Nansen to Venizelos, the Greek leader, the following day. Venizelos himself had already thought of such an exchange in 1915. The difficulty was that the Turks did not recognize Nansen's official status, nor that of the League of Nations. The idea was subsequently raised by Nansen in talks with Hamid Bey, president of the Turkish Red Crescent Organization.[5] Hamid Bey accepted that Nansen's representatives should be allowed to travel to Asia Minor to organize relief for the displaced persons in the region. Hamid Bey drew attention to about 20,000 Ottoman refugees who taken refuge in Bulgaria and 1,000 Turkish civilians who had been deported by the Greeks from Smyrna during 1921. Nansen promised to make contact with the Bulgarian and Greek Governments on these matters. There was a problem in eastern Thrace since the Turks were attempting to move all the Greek and Russian refugees who had taken refuge there in a westward direction. Nansen hoped that the Greek population of eastern Thrace would not be obliged to leave. Nansen's report of the meeting continues:

> I expressed to [Hamid Bey] my view that if they left the country at all, they should do so only as the result of a proper exchange of population arranged

between the Greek and Turkish Governments. He expressed himself as being
in entire agreement with this view and also as definitely in favour of a complete exchange of populations as and when this could be satisfactorily arranged. He was not very optimistic as to the possibility of rapid action on this
matter. . . . I formed the impression that on this matter, as on all other questions on policy, Hamid Bey was afraid of committing himself as to the policy
of his government.

Nansen proposed an unprecedented exchange of more than a million Greeks
who had been living on Turkish soil for several hundred thousand Turks
living in Greece. On 15 October Nansen formally invited the four Allied
High Commissions in Constantinople (France, Italy, Japan and the United
Kingdom) to agree to an exchange of Greek and Turkish populations.

The displaced Turks would receive full compensation for their financial
losses and a loan would enable the Greek Government to provide for the
homecoming refugees. Nansen investigated the situation in Greece and discussed with the government the raising of a major international loan so that
the refugees could become self-supporting. He wrote a report stating that a
loan of £10 million was needed and could be repaid over ten years. Finally,
in July 1923 the Council of the League of Nations agreed to award Greece a
loan of £6 million through an organization called the Greek Refugee Settlement Commission (GRSC).[6] The loan was to be paid off between 1924 and
1932. Further loans brought the final amount to £12.3 million. The possibility of giving Turkey a loan was never seriously considered. Nansen did not
play any significant role in the actual negotiations to secure these loans.

The Greek Government used the money to build houses, schools and
hospitals, to drill wells and, alongside the introduction of modern agricultural
techniques, to purchase farm animals, ploughs and seed corn. The funding
was also designed to establish industry and to purchase fishing boats in order
to boost the economy. A model refugee settlement was established in Western Thrace[7] and its success pointed the way to a solution of the larger problem. Once again Nansen was ahead of his time with his strategy "from relief
to development aid." The success of the GRSC inspired other countries to
apply for such loans, but only Bulgaria did so successfully.

NANSEN GOES TO CONSTANTINOPLE

In November 1922 Nansen went to Constantinople at the invitation of the
four Great Powers to open negotiations between the Turks and the Greeks for
an exchange of minority populations. He stayed in Constantinople for two
months. He had a sincere desire to contribute to the achievement of peace in
the Eastern Mediterranean. After an unsuccessful attempt to find a solution to

the situation in Thrace, he had presented the bold plan for the exchange of the Greek population in Turkey for the Turkish-speaking population in Greece.

Upon his arrival in Constantinople Nansen had written the following:

> There is evidence that within the last few days a large number of refugees have arrived from the Black Sea ports of Anatolia, and they all report that a great new movement of the Greeks and Armenian populations has begun. They allege that at least 100,000 Armenians and 250,000 Greeks are now moving towards the coast to take refuge in Europe. These new refugees are arriving in the same condition as the first refugees from Asia Minor, that is to say with nothing but the clothes they wear.

One week later Nansen wrote:

> In addition to the problems mentioned, there is further the possibility of a new exodus of Christian populations from Asia Minor. 3,000 Armenians from the North Coast of Asia Minor arrived recently at Constantinople, panic stricken, stating that all their males had either been killed or detained and that they themselves had the choice either of leaving within a few days or of being deported to the interior. They furthermore expressed the fear that it was the intention of the Turks to expel or exterminate the Christians in Asia Minor. Such an eventuality must be considered, and the consequent prospect of a further 300,000 Greeks and at least 100,000 Armenians being turned out of their country.

The flow of refugees continued from the coasts of Asia Minor and the Greek Government had reached the limits of the number of refugees it could accept. There was also at this time no further possibility of absorbing Armenians. Nansen found it inadmissible that such a large mass of people could be expelled from their own country and thrown upon the mercy of the world.

The refugees from Asia Minor had left their homes in such haste that they only had the summer clothes which they were wearing at the time. They were without shelter or winter clothing. Utter destitution prevailed among hundreds of thousands of refugees during the winter of 1922/1923 when they were housed in railway stations, tents, abandoned military premises and even in the open air with no provision in the way of blankets. The weakened resistance of the refugees accentuated by insufficient food and the severe winter conditions rapidly brought epidemics in their train. The mortality among babies and their mothers soon reached alarming proportions and in some refugee camps smallpox was declared. By the beginning of 1923 Nansen's staff estimated that at least 30,000 refugees had died, particularly of pneumonia. Typhoid, cholera and, above all, typhus were expected to follow, and it was imperative that immediate steps should be taken to provide every possible assistance to the Greek municipal authorities in combating these dangers. Nansen pointed out that "the shortage of food, the housing conditions, the cold from which the refugees suffer, and the lack of clothing, all increase the probability of serious epidemics."

The British offered £50,000 if it could be matched by contributions from other sources. Since only £20,000 was forthcoming, the British withdrew most of their money. The High Commissioner was fortunate to secure the co-operation of the Epidemics Commission of the League of Nations which placed the sum of £5,000 at his disposal to combat sickness among the refugees. This money was used to purchase 40,000 doses of vaccine for the inoculation of refugees against epidemic diseases. [8]

As elsewhere, the organization of Nansen's relief efforts for the Greek refugees has been described as chaotic and bordering on incompetence. In a letter dated 22 December 1922, Philip Noel-Baker indignantly rushed to Nansen's defence:

> My dear Tony,
> I was extremely surprised to receive from you a record of your cousin, Mr Watson. I know Mr Watson and like and respect him greatly. I think it's most valuable to have from him at first-hand an account on what people are saying in Athens. It will enable us to take the necessary steps to remove some of the misconceptions there and to instruct our people that they must try to do a little better propaganda. While, however I think it was kind of Mr Watson to have told you what people are saying in Athens, was it not a mistake to embody what he said in a memorandum without stepping upstairs and enquiring from Mr de Wallerville or Major Johnson whether the rumours he reported were in fact true?

Noel-Baker then tries to put the record straight about what Nansen and his team were actually doing. He ends the letter as follows: "I am sending a copy of this letter to the Secretary-General. After working for two and half years for Dr Nansen I know the dangers of mudslinging and how very hard it is to catch it up. You will therefore forgive me if I have written in a somewhat violent manner."[9]

Nevertheless, other international aid agencies considered Nansen to be impractical and refused to co-operate with him. This opposition made it very difficult for the High Commissioner to organize relief and it became a side-show to the major American and British aid organizations.

In January 1923, Nansen described to the Council of the League of Nations what he had accomplished for *all* refugees, without distinction for race or religion. Although the ICRC was very active in the Smyrna region and the Sea of Marmara, the High Commissioner for Refugees had dispatched 350 tons of flour to the area to alleviate the food crisis. He had also assisted the Turkish authorities by providing shipping in order to repatriate 10,000 Muslim refugees from Constantinople to Smyrna and other parts of Asia Minor. "Their immediate return to their homes enabled them to collect their olive crop, to plough their fields for the winter sowing and thus to become self-supporting."

AN EXCHANGE IS AGREED

Nansen's proposal for a compulsory exchange of populations was acceptable to the Great Powers because it provided a solution to an otherwise intractable problem. There was, however, a great deal of opposition in Greece, Turkey, elsewhere in Europe and the United States to the idea of a compulsory exchange of populations because, to many people, it appeared brutal—indeed it was, but it was the only realistic solution. In Nansen's report submitted to the League's Council on 2 February 1923, he states:

> In November I informed the members of the League that, while in Constantinople I had accepted an invitation from the representatives of the Principal Powers to negotiate between the Governments of Turkey and Greece for an exchange of populations and prisoners of war. In accepting this invitation I acted in accordance with what I was officially informed were the wishes of both the Governments interested. In spite of this, no great progress was made with the negotiations. . . . I was compelled to leave without reaching any conclusion. Matters had, however sufficiently progressed for me to be able to prepare a draft of a possible agreement which was left with the two governments for their consideration. When the Peace Conference met at Lausanne, I thought it my duty to propose to the representatives of the inviting parties that negotiations might be taken up again. . . . I was invited by Lord Curzon, the President of the First Conference on the subject, and I explained that I had only interested myself in this question at the invitation of the Principal Powers. . . . I urged that, if an exchange was going to take place, it should be made in time for at least a considerable proportion of the exchanged populations to be able to cultivate the land of their new farms during the coming spring. [10]

In a letter dated 6 March 1923, Noel-Baker wrote ironically to Major Johnson:

> Of course, there is an extremely good case for the view that the proper thing to do with the refugees in Greece is to send them back to Asia Minor. It was, as you know, the view with which Dr Nansen originally went to Constantinople, and he hoped to induce Kemal to agree to receive them in decent conditions, that was indeed his main motive in going. What he found there rapidly induced him to change his mind. If Colonel Haskell will induce the American Government to make the Turks change their mind and receive these people back in good conditions, and will also induce them to make the Turks accept satisfactory arrangements for their protection in their homes in the future, then he will have a real ground for objecting to the Exchange of Populations, and to settlement schemes in Greece. As there is not the least prospect that anybody will be able to make the Turks agree to any of these for at least two or three years, the

case for Exchange of Populations and finding capital to settle her refugees of
the great vacant land which she has, seems to me unanswerable.[11]

At first, both the Greeks and Turks strongly resisted the idea of an exchange
but, thanks to Nansen's persistent diplomatic efforts, he managed to get both
parties to accept the plan at the beginning of the Lausanne Peace Conference
in 1923. On 30 January 1923 Greece and Turkey signed a Convention Concerning the Exchange of Greek and Turkish Populations providing for the
compulsory exchange of national minorities. The first article of the Convention reads as follows:

> As from 1 May 1923, there shall take place a compulsory exchange of Turkish
> nationals of the Greek Orthodox religion established in Turkish territory, and
> of Greek nationals of the Moslem religion established in Greek territory.

The actual exchange of populations began on 24 July 1923, although most of
the Greek population of Turkey had already fled Anatolia by this time. It is
believed that 1.5 million Greeks and some 400,000 Turks were eventually
established in new homes.

In Nansen's report presented in September 1923, he wrote: "Immediately
after the last Assembly, the High Commissioner proceeded to Constantinople, Eastern Thrace and Athens to carry out an inquiry onto the problem of
the Near East and established close contact with the Greek and Turkish
authorities and with the leaders of the relief organizations which had begun
to bring assistance to the refugees."

Nansen goes on: "Very high tribute had to be paid to the noble work
carried out by the American Red Cross, which lost very little time in intro-
ducing measures for the feeding of the refugees and was instrumental in the
early days in saving over 800,000 refugees from literal starvation." The
American Red Cross continued its relief activities in Greece on the same
generous scale up to the end of June 1923, and even at that date it was
feeding no fewer than 500,000 refugees.

Nansen's ambitious plan took eight years to complete, but by the end of
1924 the main migrations were largely over. Although millions of people had
been obliged to leave their homes, it could be said that this operation was
carried out successfully and had two unforeseen benefits: the risk of minority
populations being oppressed had been avoided; and the Greek economy was
to benefit from a large influx of enterprising merchants.

Some idea of the scope of the growth of the international refugee problem
may gained by Nansen's report of March 1924: "The suppression of the
powers of the diplomatic and consular institutions of the former Russian
region at Constantinople has obliged the High Commission to undertake
semi-official protection of Russian refugees in Turkey." There had been

about 400,000 Armenian and Russian refugees unemployed or in temporary or casual employment in Asia Minor and the Middle East.[12]

As always, finance was the problem. Voluntary organizations such as the American relief organizations and the Save the Children Fund continued to help to their utmost with great generosity. Nansen reported again:

> Although the economic crises which have endured during the last few years have borne more heavily on the refugees than on those workers who enjoyed the protection of national governments, and have resulted in many former employment avenues being closed to the refugees, it is very satisfactory to note that the total number of unemployed Armenian and Russian refugees has now been reduced to less than 180,000. Whilst not claiming full credit for the transformation into productive members of the community of the 220,000 refugees who have thus during the last four years become self-supporting, it may be claimed that the majority of those refugees owe their improved situation, either directly or indirectly, to the various measures initiated by and executed in conjunction with the High Commission for Refugees.

THE LAUSANNE CONFERENCE

After the destruction of the Greek forces at Smyrna in Asia Minor in 1922, Turkey officially rejected the Treaty of Sèvres that had been signed by the Ottoman Government. This meant that it was necessary to start all over again with negotiating a true peace with Turkey to conclude the First World War.

In October 1922 the Western Allies issued invitations to all interested parties to attend a conference in Lausanne to settle the affairs of Asia Minor. A very imprudent error was committed when an invitation was sent to the Ottoman sultan Mehmet VI, who since August 1920 was no more than a puppet of the Allies. The Turkish Grand National Assembly in Ankara regarded this as an outrageous insult and Mustafa Kemal reacted quickly and decisively. He proposed to the Assembly the abolition of the sultanate and the expulsion of Mehmet VI—Turkey would therefore become a republic. The Assembly appointed a commission to examine the question, since conservative elements hesitated about taking such a radical step. Finally, Kemal placed his supporters with loaded revolvers behind the seated delegates and demanded an immediate decision. On 1 November 1922 they passed a law abolishing the sultanate and declaring that all power now belonged to the Grand National Assembly. The sultan was taken to Malta on board a British warship and later settled on the Italian Riviera. Thus collapsed one of the greatest empires ever known in modern history.

İsmet İnönü was the chief negotiator for Turkey during the Conference of Lausanne. Lord Curzon, the British Foreign Secretary of that time, was the chief negotiator for the Allies, while Eleftherios Venizelos represented Greece. The Allied delegation included Admiral Mark L. Bristol, who served as the United States High Commissioner—and championed the Turkish cause.

The negotiations took many months. On 20 November 1922, the conference opened and, as a result of tense debates, was interrupted by a Turkish walk-out on 4 February 1923. After reopening on 23 April, and following more protests by the Turks and further frank exchanges, the treaty was signed on 24 July—the outcome of eight months of arduous negotiations.

The treaty was composed of 143 articles with major sections including a convention on the Turkish straits, trade, agreements and binding letters. The treaty provided for the independence of the Republic of Turkey, but also for the protection of the Greek Orthodox Christian minority in Turkey and the Muslim minority in Greece. However, as we have already noted above, most of the Greek population had by this time left Turkey and the Turkish-speaking population of Greece would be deported under Nansen's Convention signed by Greece and Turkey. [13]

The treaty delimited the boundaries of Greece, Bulgaria and Turkey. Only the Greeks of Constantinople, and Imvros and Tenedos (two islands at the entrance to the Dardanelles) were excluded at that time (affecting about 270,000 people), and the Muslim population of Western Thrace (another 129,000 people). Article 14 granted the islands of Imvros and Tenedos (in Turkish, Gökçeada and Bozcaada) a "special administrative organization," a right that was revoked by the Turkish government a few years later. The Republic of Turkey also formally accepted the loss of Cyprus to the British (Article 20), which had been leased to the British Empire following the Congress of Berlin in 1878, but *de jure* remained an Ottoman territory until the First World War. The same was true of Egypt and Sudan (Article 17), which had been occupied by British forces under the pretext of "putting down the Urabi Revolt and restoring order" in 1882, but in theory remained Ottoman territories until the First World War. Turkey formally ceded all claims on Syria and Iraq (Article 3) and the boundaries of these two nations were established. The fate of the province of Mosul on the border of Turkey and Iraq was determined through a decision of the League of Nations. Turkey also renounced all claims on the Dodecanese Islands (Article 15), which reverted to Greece.

Adakale Island, the Ottoman sultan's private possession in the River Danube, had been totally overlooked during earlier peace talks at the Congress of Berlin in 1878. However, Romania unilaterally declared its sovereignty over the island in 1919 and further strengthened this claim with the Treaty of Trianon in 1920. This island no longer exists having been submerged following the construction of the Iron Gates Dams between 1964 and 1984.

The territories to the south of Syria and Iraq on the Arabian Peninsula, which still remained under Turkish control when the Armistice of Mudros was signed on 30 October 1918, were not explicitly identified in the text of the treaty. However, by the definition of Turkey's southern border in Article 3 it was evident that Turkey had officially ceded them. These territories included Yemen, Asir and parts of Hejaz like the city of Medina. They had been held by Turkish forces until January 1919.

Turkey also renounced its authority over Libya which had been defined by Article 10 of the Treaty of Ouchy in 1912 (covered by Article 22 of the Treaty of Lausanne).

The Treaty of Lausanne led to the international recognition of the sovereignty of the new Republic of Turkey as the successor state of the defunct Ottoman Empire. The Convention on the Dardanelles lasted only thirteen years and was replaced with the Montreux Convention Regarding the Regime of the Turkish Straits in 1936.

Hatay Province remained a part of the French Mandate of Syria according to the Treaty of Lausanne, but in 1938 gained its independence as the Hatay State and then joined Turkey after a referendum in 1939. Syria does not recognize the addition of Hatay Province to Turkey and continues to show it as a part of Syria on its maps.

NOTES

1. Helmreich, P.C. *From Paris to Sèvres: The Partition of the Ottoman Empire at the Peace Conference of 1919–1920,* pp. 38–46. Columbia, OH: Ohio State University Press, 1974.

2. Helmreich, pp. 290–337.

3. Minutes of the tenth meeting of the Assembly of the League of Nations, 18 September 1922, ref. 48/27750, box R–1755, League of Nations Archives.

4. Notes written by Philip Noel-Baker, ref. 48/27750, box R–1755, League of Nations Archives.

5. Dated 15 October 1922, ref. 48/24324/23548, box R–1755, League of Nations Archives.

6. Minutes of the twenty-fourth session of the Council of the League of Nations, League of Nations Archives.

7. Nansen's report to the twenty-fourth session of the Council, PVC XXIV, box R–1755, League of Nations Archives.

8. Reynolds, E.E. *Nansen,* p. 235. Harmondsworth, UK: Penguin Books, 1949.

9. Letter, 18 December 1922, ref. 25508/23548, box R–1755, League of Nations Archives.

10. Report by Nansen to the twenty-third session of the Council, 16 February 1923, ref. 48/26109/23548, box R–1755, League of Nations Archives.

11. Letter, 6 March 1923, box R–1755, League of Nations Archives.

12. Report to the twenty-fourth session of the Council, box R–1755, League of Nations Archives.

13. Helmreich, pp. 300–339.

Chapter Seven

The Nansen Passport

THE ORIGINS

In the early part of the twentieth century, more and more states were extending control over their borders by issuing national passports. By this means, governments could regulate exit, transit and entry and could control to some extent the national labour market. Ultimately, the passport became indispensable for all international travellers. In addition to easy and certain proof of identity and nationality, it gave the holder diplomatic protection and assistance. For refugees, the passport made it easier to settle in the country of immigration and to draw up official documents, such as birth certificates for the immigrant and his/her family. It enabled the holder to find work or enter into other contracts, and to qualify for social, economic and medical assistance. Finally, the passport enabled the holder to return without hindrance to the country that had originally issued the document.

The question of passports became critical after 1918. As a result of the upheavals of war and revolution, between 1 and 2 million Russian nationals fled what was eventually to become known as the Union of Soviet Socialist Republics. This uprooted band of different ethnic and religious groups— Jews, ethnic Germans and White Russian Orthodox—came from every socio-economic class, from both rural and urban areas, and from all parts of the former Russian Empire. Some found asylum in Europe, notably Poland, Czechoslovakia and Germany. Others sought sanctuary in Asia Minor. Still others escaped to China, especially to Manchuria and Shanghai. It was impossible to return these refugees to Russian territory as the Soviet Government declared that they had forfeited their Russian nationality. They were formally stripped of their citizenship by a decree dated December 1921.[1]

One problem affecting all refugees was proof of nationality. Most of them had no identity papers of any kind. They were thus placed in the dilemma of being without a legal status in the country in which they had taken refuge, and not able to go elsewhere due to the lack of travel documents. The plight of refugees was described by Michael Hansson, president of the Nansen International Office for Refugees, during his acceptance speech for the 1938 Nobel Peace Prize:

> The expulsion of the refugees is probably the most sordid chapter in their story. For the most part guilty of no crime other than that of lacking the money to establish a fixed abode—and that mainly because they are not allowed to look for work and are therefore regarded as vagrants in the eyes of the law—they are driven out of one country like infested animals only to be thrown back again from another in which they had perforce to seek refuge. They are arrested once more, and this time for a more heinous crime—the violation of the expulsion order! The hard hand of the law is laid upon them. In some countries, mercifully, the ancient principle of justice still prevails: no one shall be required to do the impossible. But other countries hold to the relentless letter of the law and condemn to prison those whom the neighbouring state has forcibly pushed back across the frontier. And so the game can go on inexorably year after year.

Individuals in such circumstances were in an abnormal situation in an international order where issues of rights, nationality and protection were becoming more stringently defined and more regularly enforced. Russian exiles were therefore condemned to unemployment and poverty because they had no valid identity. They had difficulty working in the country of their first refuge, as well as being unable to move to another country in search of a better life. On the other hand, the countries of refuge could not allow them to stay indefinitely since these nations were themselves in the throes of the economic crisis brought about by the aftermath of the First World War.

The only solution was for the refugees to migrate to countries less affected by the crisis where they had a better chance of finding employment. But, since they possessed no valid identity and travel documents, they were unable do so. Even if travel documents were issued to them by the countries where they had found temporary sanctuary, these documents in most cases did not grant them entry to the countries to which they wished to go. It was evident that something had to be done about clarifying the legal status of these refugees in their new homeland. This affected particularly the Russian and the Armenian refugees who, despite the Soviet Government stating that they would be refused entry, were in danger of being returned to the USSR against their will. The issuing of a special identity and travel document to Russian refugees was one of the problems most urgently requiring Nansen's attention.

REFINING THE MODEL

On the 21 August 1921, the Council of the League of Nations convened a meeting in Geneva in order to consider the Russian refugee problem as a whole and to adopt a series of resolutions which would serve as guiding principles for Nansen's work.

It was Édouard Frick who first suggested the need for an identity document recognized by an international agreement conferring a legal status that would spare the holder from the torments of having no nationality. The question of travel documents was examined at a series of three conferences and benefited from a wide range of expertise. The first was the conference of representatives of the governments concerned by the problem of Russian refugees in Geneva in August 1921 and actually convened by the International Labour Organisation (ILO).[2] A second conference of governmental representatives met in September 1921 with an advisory committee representing private Russian organizations. Finally, a special conference was held in Paris at which representatives of the High Commissioner for Refugees and experts appointed by various Russian organizations took part. Nansen presented his first report to the fourteenth session of the Council of the League of Nations in March 1922, and he dwelt upon the extraordinary difficulties encountered when working for Russian refugees. Following Frick's suggestion, he proposed a form of identity certificate to be issued to Russian refugees.[3]

The following day, the Council drew the attention of governments to the necessity of taking action in conformity with Nansen's proposals. The replies received from the governments were inconclusive, so the question remained pending. In consequence, the advisory committee of private relief organizations, which met again in Paris in May 1922, requested the High Commissioner to continue his efforts to find a solution to the matter of identity documents. Particularly, it asked him to summon another conference, as had been suggested by the French Government. To this end, Nansen organized another international conference that resulted in the adoption of the first legal instrument relating to the protection of refugees. The Arrangement with regard to the Issue of Certificates of Identity to Russian Refugees was signed in Geneva on 5 July 1922. Following Nansen's proposal, this conference proposed for the first time international travel documents specifically for refugees from Russia. These people were defined as "any person of Russian origin who does not enjoy the protection of the Government of the Union of Soviet Socialist Republics and who has not acquired any other nationality." This unconventional proof of identity had the advantage of avoiding any impression of formal recognition of the Soviet Government by other European countries, as well as circumventing the subject of its policy of depriving refugees of their Russian citizenship.

The idea was that special identity certificates for Russian refugees would be issued by the authorities of the country in whose territory they resided. The report of the conference included a model of a specimen passport, which was based on identity documents issued by the German and Czech authorities. This document, afterwards commonly called the "Nansen Passport," was not legally binding but suggested a recommended standard. It would be issued annually stating the holder's identity, nationality and race, and therefore provided some freedom of movement. With this document the holder could move from one country to another to find work or to rejoin family members, but it did not replace a national passport because it did not give the holder the automatic right of return to the country that issued the documents without a special provision to that effect. On 11 August 1922, the Secretary-General of the League of Nations invited member states to prepare such identity documents according to Nansen's model and to recognize those issued by other governments. It was recommended that countries adopting the arrangement should notify him of their intentions at the earliest possible date. The Nansen Passport represented the first in a long and still evolving series of international legal measures designed to protect refugees. Strangely, Czechoslovakia, which had been the driving force in placing this matter on the agenda, rejected the Nansen Passport on the grounds that its actual arrangements were entirely adequate.

The Council of the League decided that the Nansen Passport had now come into existence and asked governments to signify their official acceptance.[4] None of the governments that had participated in the conference to examine the High Commissioner's proposals expressed its acceptance—in so many words. There are therefore no official instruments signed by the representatives of governments. However, governments could adhere to it simply through a formal declaration addressed to the Secretary-General of the League.

The main provisions of the agreement were that "the certificate was to be issued to the Russian refugees who should apply for it." In this respect the arrangement took into consideration a memorandum submitted by a group of Russian lawyers, who maintained that the identity document should be issued only to those refugees who applied for it of their own accord. It would not be compulsory for refugees who already possessed proper documents guaranteeing them all the necessary facilities. The certificate should not infringe the laws and regulations in force in each state concerning the control of foreigners. It should not in any way affect special regulations with regard to persons of Russian nationality, including those who had lost that nationality without acquiring another. The state which issued the certificate was alone qualified to renew it as long as the refugee concerned continued to reside within its borders. The certificate would cease to be valid if the bearer at any time entered Russian territory. The arrangement allowed the bearers to enter another country if the authorities of that country affixed their entry visa directly on the document. It also stipulated that countries would grant transit visas, subject to the regulations in force in these states and on condition that the refugees had obtained the visa of the country of final destination.

The text of the certificate was to be in at least two languages: the national language of the issuing authority and the French language, as laid down by the Paris Conference of 21 October 1920. The certificate was to be issued free of charge on demand, except in the event of legal requirements to the contrary in a particular country. Finally, and this was one of the most important features of the arrangements actually adopted in July 1922—and one which greatly diminished the value of the original Nansen Passport compared with national passports—the possession of the passport did not in any way imply the refugee's automatic right of return. A refugee who left the country in which the certificate had been issued could not re-enter the country unless special permission to do so had been granted and included on the document. This problem was specifically addressed in 1924 by the addition of a phrase recommending that the right of return be authorized "whenever possible."

The third annual Assembly of the League of Nations meeting in September 1922 approved the procedures set up in favour of Russian refugees and requested the Council to draw the attention of member States to the importance of this matter. By 1923 thirty-nine governments recognized the right of holders of the Nansen Passport to cross international borders, thus facilitating the more equitable distribution of Russian refugees. The American journalist Dorothy Thompson wrote in 1938: "The Nansen certificate is the greatest things that had happened to the individual refugee. It returned to him his lost identity." One by one, fifty-four countries accepted it. The acceptance of the Nansen Passport by one country in particular must be mentioned—Germany, a country which was not a League member at that time, but which had granted refuge to several hundred thousand Russian refugees. Note should also be taken of Turkey's attitude, since it had been responsible for generating a large number of refugees. At first this country refused to approve the Nansen Passport, but by 1925 the Turkish Government felt comfortable with the wording of the document and accepted it.

A special body was required to provide assistance to refugees. The ILO Refugee Service was created and chaired by one of Nansen's former assistants, Thomas Frank Johnson. Between 1925 and 1929 this service would assist the High Commissioner in providing employment, transport and accommodation for refugees. At the same time, it would make the refugees less vulnerable.

When negotiations with the USSR about the repatriation of Russian refugees failed, Nansen spearheaded the adoption of additional measures to provide a secure legal position in their host countries. His efforts led to the adoption in June 1928 of two important legal instruments, namely the Arrangement relating to the Legal Status of Russian and Armenian Refugees and the Arrangement concerning the Extension to other Categories of Refugees of Certain Measures taken in Favour of Russian and Armenian Refugees. The legal status of refugees was therefore extended to new groups of displaced people: Armenian, Turkish, Assyrian and Assyro-Chaldean. Thanks to Nansen's efforts, between 1922 and 1926 various international agreements would lead to the clarification of the status of refugee. These early legal agreements later became the basis on which subsequent refugee law was founded. They were codified and supplemented by the Geneva Convention relating to the Status of Refugees of 28 July 1951, which constitutes the main instrument in the world today for the protection of displaced persons.[5]

Nansen had already lent his name to various charitable initiatives, but some of the passports actually carried not only his name but a portrait of the famous man. This was, no doubt, Nansen's greatest legacy. He ministered to hundreds of thousands of refugees utilizing the methods that were to become classic: custodial care, repatriation, rehabilitation, resettlement, emigration, integration. Among the illustrious Russian émigrés who benefited from this arrangement were Igor Stravinsky, Marc Chagall, Anna Pavlova and Sergei Rachmaninoff.

EMPLOYMENT FOR REFUGEES

By the middle of 1924 the political difficulties of the refugees had mostly been resolved and the problem had become one of finding employment. Nansen started negotiations with all countries that he thought might be willing to accept refugees and give them employment.[6] Many governments resisted because at that time they were struggling with their own problems of unemployment in a period of economic recession. He had to negotiate with the authorities in country after country, working closely with the ILO in finding suitable employment for refugees.

Nansen felt that the ILO was the most appropriate organization to deal with the complicated questions of work and emigration, and which was also likely to avoid the exploitation of the refugees.[7] This possibility was discussed in the League's Council meetings and the task was indeed taken over by the ILO in 1925 as far as technical problems were involved. Nansen was left to deal with other matters, particularly political and legal questions which did not come within the sphere of the ILO. By the time technical matters were transferred to the ILO, a large number of refugees had succeeded in becoming self-supporting thanks to the Nansen Passport and other measures initiated by the High Commissioner. An arrangement of 1928 permitted the representatives of the High Commissioner to exercise important consular functions, certifying the identity of refugees and their status according to international law.[8]

Meanwhile, countries with significant numbers of refugees were spending huge sums of money on providing day-to-day support for them. The staff of the High Commissioner for Refugees estimated that this money would be more efficiently spent if it were not used for short-term relief but for long-term settlement and employment. However, when Nansen and ILO Director-General Albert Thomas proposed establishing a revolving fund of £100,000, the response was very modest. The ILO did eventually succeed in establishing a revolving fund with the help of private contributions under Nansen's trusteeship from which transport expenses could be advanced to refugees. They undertook to repay them when they became established in their new home. It was an intergovernmental agreement of 1926 that established a fee of five gold francs (equivalent to five Swiss francs) for each issue or renewal of the Nansen Passport. In this way, refugees were able to contribute to their own settlement. In other words, it was the refugees themselves who covered the greater part of the cost. Meanwhile, the sale of postage stamps issued by both the Norwegian and French Governments in aid of the refugees produced good results. The response in Norway was particularly substantial when measured in proportion to this country's small population. Voluntary gifts also played their part. Funds were sometimes used in the form of loans to encourage self-help, although the refugees were not always able to repay them. In a number of countries, refugee organizations were able to request national subsidies in such a way as to double or even treble the sums originally received.

As of 1 January 1925, the High Commissioner's staff was incorporated into the Diplomatic Division of the ILO as its "Refugee Service." The High Commissioner's Office would, however, continue to exist as a separate entity and remain responsible for the legal status of refugees.[9] Between 1925 and 1929 the Director-General of the ILO reported that approximately 400,000 unemployed refugees fell under its mandates. Some 200,000 had found an occupation during these years, and the ILO could claim direct credit for having contributed to finding employment for over 50,000 of them, mainly as agricultural workers. Despite these achievements, in 1929, the collaboration between Nansen and the ILO came to an end. This was in part due to the fact that many of the refugees who remained unemployed were not agricultural workers and the task of finding employment for them became more complicated. It was also due to the fact that the League now considered it essential to consolidate legal protection arrangements and to come to a definite solution to the refugee question. The humanitarian aspect of refugee work was entrusted to the International Refugee Office, which later became known as the Nansen International Office for Refugees in commemoration if the High Commissioner who had died in May 1930.

Nansen ministered to a multitude of refugees utilizing the methods that were to become the basis of present international regime for the protection of refugees. To this end he set up a whole organisation for buying food, chartering transport and raising the necessary funds. He established the basic structure of what would in 1950 become the Office of the United Nations High Commissioner for Refugees.

One of the most striking features of this process was the enormous amount of good that could be achieved by the most modest contribution. Many a small donation enabled the head of a family to take up a trade or start a small business. People were prepared to live on meagre resources when necessity demanded—how great is human fortitude in desperate circumstances!

THE NANSEN PASSPORT IN PRACTICE

But what of other groups of refugees? In fact, there were 320,000 Armenian refugees scattered throughout various countries, particularly in Greece and Syria, the survivors of political and religious persecutions in Turkey. They did not have any identity documents either. Following a request received from the Armenian National Delegation, on 28 September 1923 the Council of the League asked the High Commissioner for Refugees to examine the question of granting identity to these people. In order to give effect to this, on 31 May 1924 Nansen submitted a plan for creating an identity certificate for Armenian refugees. This model was largely a reproduction of the arrangement made for the Russian refugees, with some slight modifications. It included a more favourable attitude to the refugees—the certificate would be valid for two years, and to the very important question of the right to return there was also a small change. In this way the Council of the League of Nations extended the benefits of the Nansen Passport to Armenian refugees. In an intergovernmental conference held in 1926, Armenian refugees were defined as "any person of Armenian origin, formerly a subject of the Ottoman Empire, who does not enjoy the protection of the Government of the Turkish Republic and who has not acquired any other nationality."

Nevertheless, in actual practice the system established by these arrangements was found to possess a number of shortcomings resulting in some absurd situations. For example: for no particular reason some countries stipulated that passports could or could not be issued to those who had entered a country or wished to leave by a given (i.e. arbitrary) date; children could not be listed on their parents' passports; the documents were only valid for one year; the fees for a Nansen Passports were higher than for a national passport; in some cases countries insisted on the authorization of the Soviet authorities before issuing a passport! Following a resolution by the sixth session of the Assembly of the League of Nations (1925), the Council requested the High Commissioner for Refugees to convene an intergovernmental conference with a view to making the amendments which experience had shown to be necessary. This conference, which was attended by delegates of twenty-five governments, met in Geneva on 10 May 1926, and drew up an arrangement subsequently adopted by twenty-three of these governments. This specified the following point in particular:

> It has been seen that the Nansen certificate did not confer on the holder the right to return to the country where the certificate had been issued unless this right of return was expressly mentioned on the document. However, the experience of the previous years had shown that many States were unwilling to affix entrance visas on documents which did not guarantee the holder's right of return, and in consequence the free movement of refugees seeking a place of permanent settlement in Europe was restricted.

The arrangement of 1926 put an end to this situation by means of a statement which differed entirely from the corresponding clauses of 1922 and 1924, but the validity of the passport was still limited to one year.

A further milestone in the protection of refugees was made in 1933 with the Refugee Convention becoming international law. Particularly important was the clause on "non-refoulement," which meant that a refugee could not be expelled or returned, against his or her will, to a territory where there was a risk of persecution. It was finally in 1951 that the United Nations adopted the Convention relating to the Status of Refugees as the key legal document defining who is a refugee, their rights and the legal obligations of states.

THE NOBEL PEACE LAUREATE

On 10 December 1922 Nansen was awarded the Nobel Peace Prize for his efforts in favour of the prisoners of war, famine relief, the Russian refugees and the population movements in Asia Minor. Although the Nobel prizes for physics, physiology, chemistry, literature and medicine are awarded by Swedish institutions, the peace prize is presented by the Norwegian Parliament or Storting. When he learned that he had been honoured with this award, Nansen immediately wrote to Philip Noel-Baker indicating that in many ways he owed his status as an international statesman to his faithful assistant. "All I have done in the League and for the League has been done with you, and could not have been done without you, at least in the manner it was achieved."

Nansen also gave thought to the provision of long-term assistance to help the Russian people to help themselves once the direct effects of privation were over. Noel-Baker was alarmed to learn that Nansen intended spending some of his Nobel Prize money (about £24,000) on famine relief in Russia, although the Russian authorities themselves said that the famine was over.

Nevertheless, after visiting Moscow again, Nansen decided to use some of the money to set up two model farms, one in the Volga region and another one in the Ukraine. These new schemes involved importing farm machinery and this is believed to be the first time that tractors were employed in Russian farming. At one stage Nansen's son Kåre was employed as a forestry expert on the model farm in the Volga region. After a year or so the model farms collapsed.

In his book *Russia and Peace* (1923) Nansen justified the Bolshevik regime in Russia, although it added fuel to the idea that he was a Soviet sympathiser. This is particularly incongruous since in Norway he was known as a conservative strongly opposed to communism. In January 1925 a new conservative political party, *Fædrelandslaget*, was formed in Norway and Nansen spoke in support of it at the first rally in Oslo—Christiana was now known again by its mediaeval name. On several occasions, *Fædrelandslaget* attempted unsuccessfully to form a Norwegian Government with Nansen as prime minister. Both in Norway and at the League of Nations in Geneva, Nansen would be revered as a symbol of integrity but would fail as a politician.

Nansen remained a prominent member of the Assembly of the League of Nations from 1920 to 1929. With the exception of the first year when Francis Hagerup was in charge, he was always chairman of the Norwegian delegation. In 1928 and 1929 the Norwegian delegation included the Head of State and Foreign Minister Johan Ludwig Mowinckel and both he and Nansen signed the delegation's report. Since Mowinckel did not stay for the entire Assembly and since it had been established practice for some years, it may be assumed that Nansen remained chairman.

Nansen's particular contribution was that humanitarian work, which had previously been the domain of private organizations, now became a matter of concern to international organizations. His humanitarian work is an excellent example of how international relationships and the accumulation of expertise and experience exceeded the boundaries of nation-states.

Nansen displayed the characteristics of a charismatic leader: he was an articulate speaker who set out to influence people's behaviour; he was a wilful demagogue with a passion and moral conviction for certain issues; he was a visionary who introduced innovative approaches to problems. In the 1920s, Nansen and the French politician Aristide Briand became the high priests of international organizations.

By 1929 Nansen's health was visibly failing and his marriage to Sigrun also made both of them miserable. At the age of 67 Nansen fell in love with Brenda Ueland, an American feminist and journalist, thirty years his junior. By this time he was suffering from phlebitis, cataracts and had already experienced a heart attack in 1928. In February 1930 he went skiing with two old friends in the Norwegian mountains, one of whom was suffering from 'flu. Inevitably, Nansen caught the 'flu and was ordered to bed, being visited at home by King Haakon VII in person. After spending several weeks confined to bed, Nansen died suddenly of a heart attack on 13 May 1930. He was given a state funeral, including two minutes' silence and flags flying at half-mast. Among his pall-bearers were Philip Noel-Baker, Otto Sverdrup and Oluf Dietrichson, the latter two of whom had been with him on the Greenland expedition. Sverdrup had subsequently been the captain of the *Fram*.

NOTES

1. Hieronymi, O. The Nansen passport: A Tool of Freedom of Movement and of Protection. *Refugee Survey Quarterly*, 22/1, 2003.
2. Minutes of the fourteenth session of the Council of the League of Nations.
3. Report by Nansen to the fourteenth session of the Assembly of the League of Nations, 15 September 1922 (ref. C124.M.74).
4. Minutes of the twenty-ninth session of the Council of the League of Nations.
5. Chetail, V. Fridtjof Nansen and the International Protection of Refugees: An introduction, *Refugee Survey Quarterly*, 22/1, 2003.
6. Sorensen, J. *The Saga of Fridtjof Nansen*, p. 285. London: George Allen & Unwin, 1932.
7. Reynolds, E.E. *Nansen*. Harmondsworth, UK: Penguin Books, [1949].
8. Marrus, M. *The Unwanted: European Refugees in the Twentieth Century*. Oxford, UK: Oxford University Press, 1988.
9. Roversi, A. The Evolution of the Refugees Regime and Institutional Responses: Legacy from the Nansen Period. *Refugee Survey Quarterly*, 22/1, 2003.

Chapter Eight

Nansen's Heritage

When Nansen began his great task in favour of refugees, he believed that the problem could be solved within a period of ten years and work did indeed advance rapidly at first. This was because it was relatively easy to arouse people's pity for the refugees' plight, and also because several countries short of labour gladly opened their doors to them. But then came the economic depression beginning in 1929 and reaching its nadir in 1932. Nations surrounded themselves with strong defences by restricting imports of foreign goods and imposing immigration barriers. Now nobody wanted to accept refugees; on the contrary, everybody suddenly wanted them to leave since the national labour force had to be protected against unemployment. Refugees lived in permanent insecurity hounded from country to country because they did not benefit from diplomatic or consular protection.

When Nansen died, it was estimated then that there were still 1,100,000 homeless refugees in Europe and the Near East. For the most part these were Russians who had fled their country after the Revolution of 1917, with a second wave following the failure of the so-called White Generals' Revolt against the Soviets. There were also several hundred thousand Armenians who had lost their homes in Turkey as a result of forced deportation and fleeing massacres, both during and after the First World War.

The Nansen International Office for Refugees was established in 1931 by the League of Nations, shortly after the death of Fridtjof Nansen. It was thus the continuation of the High Commission for Refugees, established by the League of Nations on 27 June 1921 under the direction of Nansen. The Nansen International Office was established as an autonomous institution, with humanitarian aims, and was to offer the refugees all the material support that its funds would permit, including political and legal protection. The League of Nations also provided the administrative expenses for the Nansen

Passport, since its revenues for welfare and relief were obtained from private contributions. The League of Nations Secretariat left all refugee work almost entirely to the Nansen International Office, which was awarded the Nobel Peace Prize in 1938, demonstrating the enormous importance of the refugee problem.

The Nansen International Office was beset by overwhelming problems during its existence—among them, the lack of stable and adequate financing; the onset of the depression which closed employment opportunities for refugees; the decline of the prestige of the League of Nations after its failure to intervene in Manchuria in 1931 and Ethiopia in 1935; the growing avalanche of refugees, mostly from Germany, Italy and Spain; and the reluctance of member states to permit the League of Nations to intervene on behalf of persons who had previously been citizens of their countries. Particularly, the flood of people fleeing the totalitarian regimes in Germany and Spain led to the whole system breaking down, accompanied by a complete loss of faith in the League of Nations.

The funds at the disposal of the Nansen Office at the time of its creation were insignificant, but they were substantially augmented, partly by a contribution from the British Government and partly by a donation of 250,000 Norwegian kroner from Nansen's estate. This amount no doubt represented the balance, with interest, of the Peace Prize that Nansen himself had received in 1921, and of an equivalent sum given to him by the Danish publisher and philanthropist Christian Erichsen. Some of this money had been used by Nansen to set up model farms in Russia after the famine.

However, the needs were so great that the resources of the Nansen Office dwindled rapidly. The situation was helped by the intergovernmental agreement of 1926 which stipulated that the document commonly called the Nansen Passports be subject to a levy of five gold francs for each issue or renewal. One by one countries adopted this system, and the fee became the most important source of revenue for the Nansen Office. In other words, it was the refugees themselves who covered the greater part of the cost of the humanitarian work carried out by the Nansen Office. The sale of stamps by both the Norwegian and French Governments in aid of refugees also produced revenue.

A large proportion of the Office's funds were used in the form of loans to encourage self-help, and although the refugees were naturally not always able to repay the loans, these annual payments also contributed to the budget of the Nansen Office.

The most important international agreement concerning refugees was the Convention relating to the Status of Refugees adopted in Geneva by an intergovernmental conference on 28 October 1933, and ratified by Belgium, Bulgaria, Czechoslovakia, Denmark, France, Italy, Norway and the United Kingdom. Although in the first place the agreement was ratified by only these eight nations, it was in practice respected by many others. Signatory states agreed not to expel refugees possessing residence permits except in cases where national security or public order was at stake. Even then, in principle, they could not deport them unless another country was willing to accept them. The Refugee Convention—a modest charter of human rights— led to the resettlement of the Saar refugees in Paraguay after 1935; the construction of villages to house upwards of 40,000 Armenians in Syria and Lebanon; and the resettlement of another 10,000 in Yerevan. But, most importantly, it permitted material, legal and financial help to almost a million refugees.

Partly because of emigration overseas, partly because of naturalization, but also partly because of mortality among the homeless, the number of refugees under the care of the Nansen Office gradually fell to just under half a million.

The problem of German refugees after the nazis came to power in Germany became so acute in 1933 that the League of Nations established a High Commission for Refugees Coming from Germany. This Commission, whose mandate was later broadened to take in both Austrian and Sudetenland refugees, was scheduled to close on 31 December 1938, at the same time as the Nansen Office. On that date both offices were, in fact, dissolved, and the next day a new agency of the League of Nations, the Office of the High Commissioner for Refugees under the Protection of the League was opened, with headquarters in London.

At the time of the demise of the League of Nations and the formation of the United Nations, the international community was facing another refugee crisis at the end of the Second World War. The United Nations Relief and Rehabilitation Administration was established in 1944 to address the millions of people displaced across Europe as a result of the war, but replaced in 1947 by the International Refugee Organization (IRO) also founded by the United Nations. In the late 1940s, the IRO fell out of favour, but the United Nations agreed that a body was required to oversee global refugee issues. Following many heated debates in the General Assembly, the Office of the United Nations High Commissioner for Refugees (UNHCR) was founded in December 1949. The present headquarters was established on 14 December 1950 in Geneva by the United Nations General Assembly with a three-year mandate to complete its work and then disband. At no time has the work of UNHCR become unnecessary.

It has been observed that the adoption of a liberal policy on immigration has often proved profitable to host countries in the long run. Experience has shown that immigration, especially when it takes place gradually, far from harming a country, has instead provided a long-term source of energy and wealth. The United States offers the most striking example. The United Kingdom also owes its strength at least in part to its capacity to absorb foreign elements, including Jews in the 1930s. Most of the refugees given asylum have been adult people fully capable of working, whose youthful training has already been paid for by their mother country.

That is how Fridtjof Nansen understood the situation. He saw his work as a real contribution to peace. So too did the League of Nations, and when Fridtjof Nansen died the Assembly paid solemn tribute to his memory for his efforts "to unite the nations in work for the cause of peace."

Chronology

1861 Fridtjof Nansen born 10 October at Store Frøen near Christiana.

1880 Matriculation examination.

1881 Student of Zoology.

1882 March–June on board the sealer *Viking;* August appointed curator of Bergen Museum.

1884 Travels from Voss to Christiana and back on skis.

1886 Travels to Italy and studies at the research station at Naples.

1888 Doctorate. May–September Greenland expedition. Overwinters at Godthåb.

1889 Appointed to Zoological Institute, Christiana. Marries Eva Sars.

1893 Departure of the *Fram,* 24 June.

1895 Dash for the Pole — reaches 86°14′N.

1896 Meets Jackson 17 June on Franz Josef Land.

1897 Professor of Zoology at Christiana University. Edits the book of the *Fram* Expedition. Lecture tours.

1900 Studies oceanography.

1906–1908 Norwegian Ambassador to the United Kingdom

1907 Eva Nansen dies.

1908 Relinquishes ambassadorial post and becomes Professor of Oceanography.

1912 Travels to Spitsbergen.

1913 Trip to Siberia.

1917 Travels to Washington to negotiate food supplies for Norway.

1919 President of the Norwegian Union for the League of Nations. In Paris for the Peace Conference. Marries Sigrun Munthe.

1920 Norwegian delegate to the League of Nations. Accepts the role of High Commissioner for Prisoners-of-War.

1921 Accepts the role of High Commissioner for Russian Refugees and Relief Work for Famine in the Ukraine.

1922 Lecture tours collecting money for famine relief. Relief work for Greek and Armenian refugees. Nobel Peace Prize.

1923–1924 Travels to the United States and Canada. Commissioner for the Economic Construction of Greece.

1925 Travels to Armenia and the Caucasus as leader of the commission.

1926 Rector of St Andrew's University.

1928 Travels to the United States on behalf of the Armenians.

1929 Lecturing in the United States.

1930 Nansen dies 13 May. State funeral.

Bibliography

The following documents were consulted in the Archives of the League of Nations:
Fonds Mixte: Fonds des refugiés (known as the "Fonds Nansen"):

Section 40: "General"

- Box R–1574
- Box R–1575
- Box R–1576

Section 42: "Prisoners of War"

- Box R–1702
- Box R–1703
- Box R–1706

Section 45: "Russian Refugees" 1919–1927

- Box R–1713
- Box R–1719
- Box R–1728
- Box R–1729
- Box R–1744
- Box R–1748

Section 47: "Famine in Russia"

- Box R–1752
- Box R–1753.

1921. The Records of the second Assembly. Plenary Meetings.

1922.C.736(a) M.447(a). Report_Dt_Nansen_(Off. Jour.18.11.1922)

1922.C.736.M.447. Report_Dt_Nansen_(Off. Jour.15.11.1922)

1922.C.300._Nansen_Famine_en_Russie

1924. C.249. Russian Refugees. Report by F. Nansen

1924. Compte rendu financier de l'activité du Haut Commissariat Dr. F. Nansen et de l'action du Dr. F. Nansen pour le secours à la Russie de Septembre 1921 au 15 Juillet 1924, date de sa clôture. Geneva, Switzerland: League of Nations.

1924.Council_Meeting_30._Refugee_questions._Dr_Nansen_Report.

1926. Greek Refugee Settlement.

1927. Refugees Service: Dr. Nansen's Report to the eighth Assembly of the League of Nations.

1928.Refugees Service: Dr. Nansen's Report of the Council of the League of Nations.

Armenian Refugees — Request for Information re Moral Value of a Nansen Passport: Garbis Simonian, Leysin.

Armenian Refugees — Mission to South Russia and Erivan — Dr. Nansen's Report and Reports of Mr. Dupuis, Mr. Carle, Mr. Lo Savio.

Armenian Refugees — Dr. Nansen's Report — Distribution.

Collaboration of Dr. Nansen's Organisation with the League Commission of Enquiry into the Deportation of Women and Children.

Dr. Nansen's Report of the High Commissariat for the Refugees to the Governing Body of the ILO and the Council of the LON concerning the Extension of Competence of the ILO to deal with Categories of Refugees other than Russians and Armenians.

F. Nansen' s Prisoners Repatriation Account.

Issue of Nansen Passports and Identity Certificates to Other Categories of Refugees — Request of the Comité unifié d'emigration juive.

Nomination of Dr Nansen as High-Commissioner.

Relief Work done by Dr. Nansen for Turkish Refugees.

Starvation in Russia — Communications from Dr. Nansen.

Other Books Consulted

Barros, J. *An Office without Power: Secretary-General Sir Eric Drummond, 1919–33*. Oxford, UK: Oxford University Press, 1979.

Cecil, Lord Robert. *A Great Experiment: An Autobiography*. New York, NY: Oxford University Press, 1941.

Chetail, V. Fridtjof Nansen and the International Protection of Refugees: An introduction, *Refugee Survey Quarterly*, 22/1, 2003.

Fisher, H.H. *The Famine in Soviet Russia 1919–1923: The Operations of the American Relief Administration.* New York, NY: MacMillan, 1927.

Fosse, M.; Fox, J. *The League of Nations: From Collective Security to Global Rearmament.* New York, NY: United Nations, 2012.

Grahl-Madsen, A. The League of Nations and the Refugees. *A WR Bulletin* (Association for the Study of World Refugee Problems, University of Michigan), *20:*86, 1982.

Helmreich, P.C. *From Paris to Sèvres: The Partition of the Ottoman Empire at the Peace Conference of 1919–1920.* Columbia, OH: Ohio State University Press, 1974.

Hieronymi, O. The Nansen passport: A Tool of Freedom of Movement and of Protection. *Refugee Survey Quarterly*, 22/1, 2003.

Holborn, L.W. The League of Nations and the Refugee Problem. *Annals of the American Academy of Political and Social Science, 203*:124–135, 1939.

Hollander, P. *Anti-Americanism: Critiques at Home and Abroad.* New York, NY: Oxford University Press, 1992.

Hoover, H. *The Memoirs of Herbert Hoover. Years of Adventure 1874–1920.* New York, NY: Macmillan, 1951.

Hoover, H. *The Ordeal of Woodrow Wilson.* New York, Toronto & London: McGraw-Hill, 1958.

Huntford, R. *Nansen: The Explorer as Hero.* London: Abacus, 2001.

Johnston, R.H. *New Mecca New Babylon: Paris and the Russian Exiles, 1920–1945.* Montreal, Canada: McGill-Queen's University Press, 1988.

League of Nations. *Essential Facts about the League of Nations.* Geneva, Switzerland: LoN Information Section, 1939.

Lloyd George, D. *Through Terror to Triumph: Speeches and Pronouncements of the Right Hon. David Lloyd George, M.P., Since the Beginning of the War.* London: Hodder & Stoughton, 1915.

Loescher, G. *Beyond Charity: International Cooperation and the Global Refugee Crisis.* New York, NY: Oxford University Press, 1993.

MacMillan, M. *Paris 1919: Six Months That Changed the World.* New York, NY: Random House, 2003.

Marrus, M. *The Unwanted: European Refugees in the Twentieth Century.* Oxford, UK: Oxford University Press, 1988.

Metzger, B.H.M. The League of Nations and Refugees: The Humanitarian Legacy of Fridtjof Nansen. In: *The League of Nations 1920–1940. Organization and Accomplishments. A Retrospective of the First Or-*

ganization for the Establishment of World Peace, ch. 14, p. 74–80. New York & Geneva: United Nations, 1996.

Nansen, F. *The Fridtjof Nansen Memorial Lectures 1990*. Oslo: Ministry of Foreign Affairs, [1991].

Nansen. F. *The First Crossing of Greenland*. New York: Longmans, Green, 1895.

Nansen, F. *Farthest North: The Epic Adventure of a Visionary Explorer*. New York, NY: Skyhorse Publishing, 2008. [Originally published in 1897.]

Nansen, F. *Nansens røst: artikler og taler/av Fridtjof Nansen, 1884–1905*. Oslo: Jacob Dybwads Forlag, 1942. (Edited by A.H. Winsnes.)

Reynolds, E.E. *Nansen*. Harmondsworth, UK: Penguin Books, [1949].

Roversi, A. The Evolution of the Refugees Regime and Institutional Responses: Legacy from the Nansen Period. *Refugee Survey Quarterly*, 22/1, 2003.

Smuts, J.C. *The League of Nations: A Practical Suggestion*. London: Hodder & Stoughton, 1918.

Sorensen, J. *The Saga of Fridtjof Nansen*. London: George Allen & Unwin, 1932.

Vogt, C.E. *Nestekjærlighet som realpolitik Fridtjof Nansens humanitære og internasjonale prosjekt 1920–1930*. (In press.)

Whittaker, D.J. *Fighter for Peace: Philip Noel-Baker 1889–1982*. York, UK: William Sessions of York, 1989.

Index